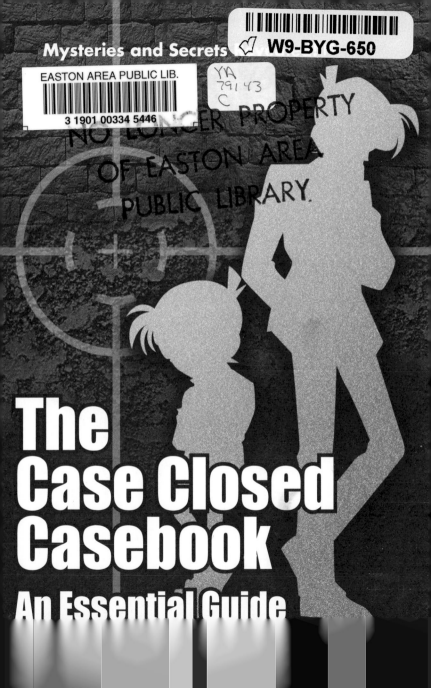

The Case Closed Casebook

An Essential Guide

cocoro books

www.dhp-online.com

cocoro books is an imprint of DH Publishing, Inc.

First Published 2008

Text and illustrations ©2008 by DH Publishing, Inc.

Compiled by Takuya Furukawa, Tim Gene

ISBN: 978-1-932897-30-2

The Case Closed Casebook: An Essential Guide

How to Use
In this book, the 19th in the popular Mysteries and Secrets Revealed! anime sourcebook series, you'll find everything you need to know about Case Closed and much, much more! And it's so easy to use. Just follow the Conan code below and within a few hours you'll be an expert investigator.

Questions and Answers
Want to find out why who did what when and where? Then this is the book for you. Continue reading and you'll find 59 Q&As on every Case Closed topic, from the Phantom Thief Kid to Professor Agasa's many weird inventions.

Glossary
When you know who's who and what's what, everything is so much easier. At the back of this book you'll find a comprehensive glossary of the many Case Closed characters and organizations, as well as an overview of every case Conan has been involved in.

Keyword Index
Want to go straight to the restaurant Columbo? Then start at the alphabetical Keyword Index at the back of this book. There you'll find page links to every character and destination in Conan's world.

CONTENTS

Introduction to Case Closed

Mystery stories are popular in Japan, but usually only in film or novels. While comics have tried to find mass appeal with whodunits, they tended to only cater to older audiences and never became big hits. Topics in comic mysteries may have been considered too violent or complicated to appeal to children, and so little energy was spent on mystery comics for kids.

This changed when Shonen Magazine published Kindaichi Case Files in 1992, which became a fast favorite of boys in high school and college. Naturally, other comic magazines quickly added kids mystery to their lineup, hoping to cash in on the new craze. Weekly Shonen Sunday, a longtime rival of Shonen Magazine, released Case Closed (Detective Conan) in 1994, but it was originally considered nothing more than a copycat series, like so many others of the time.

Case Closed proved itself, because it outlived both the famous Kindaichi Case Files and all other imitators. By 2003, Case Closed had more than 100 million copies in print, making it as popular as other landmark series like Dragon Ball.

So what makes Case Closed so special?

1. Real Detective Stories

By drawing on the traditions of mystery classics by Sir Arthur Conan Doyle, Agatha Christie, Rampo Edogawa and many more, Cased Closed creator Gosho Aoyama crafts clever and intricate stories for readers of all ages. He even introduces detectives from these stories into his own works, using otherwise obscurely known characters to bring his passion for mystery and its tradition to his readers.

Case Closed pays homage to mystery classics without stealing ideas from them, and stays original and fresh with technique and execution worthy of the best mystery novels. Tricks and foreshadowing are creative and surprising even to the most seasoned mystery fans, and all based on the plausibility of real life.

Even though the idea of a young crime-fighting detective transformed into an elementary school student seems a bit farfetched, every episode of the series is so believable that it can be enjoyed by young and old alike.

2. Series Longevity

Wherever he goes, Conan Edogawa gets pulled into a mystery, but always unravels it in no time with his amazing skills, even if he has to manipulate the adults around him to get the job done. No matter what he gets caught up in, he's always looking for answers about the people who changed him into a child, a shadowy group known only as the "Black Organization."

In the 13 years since the series started, the true nature of the Black Organization has been made clear to readers through hints and clues. Dangerous and secretive, their web reaches to all corners of the globe, and each episode reveals them as more and more of a threat. Every encounter with the Black Organization opens doors, bringing important players like the CIA and FBI into the thickening plot.

3. Endearing Characters

The character design for Case Closed is rooted in the traditional styles of boy's comics; rounded, cute, and appealing to everyone. Personalities that pair great intellect and deductive ability with romantic awkwardness and kind hearts make for characters that are easy to relate to and care for.

Kogoro Mori is most often comic relief, but despite clowning around, he comes through in a pinch and takes the spotlight for his own from time to time. Characters are more complex than they first appear, finding depth beyond stereotypes.

It wouldn't be wrong to say that Case Closed is serious mystery acted out with cute characters. By embracing these contrasts, the series appeals to all kinds of people.

Let's take a closer look at the world of Case Closed.

Chapter 01

The master detective and his friends

01   *Who is the main character?*

lways seen in big round glasses and a bow tie, Conan Edogawa lives in Beikacho, a fictional Tokyo district in Tokyo. Outwardly, he seems very innocent and childlike, but occasionally demonstrates an intelligence far above that of a six-year-old boy. In reality, he is Shinichi Kudo, a 17-year-old high school student and son of the great detective Yusaku Kudo.

It all starts with a trip to an amusement park. Shinichi and his childhood friend Ran Mori ride a roller-coaster and witness another rider's death by decapitation. Though Shinichi quickly solves the murder, for it was no accident, he stumbles across two mysterious men blackmailing a company president to keep illicit handgun sales from going public.

Shinichi is soon found out, and after the two men abduct him and discover his identity, they decide to kill him then and there. To avoid detection and making a scene, they dose him with enough of an experimental poison to kill

a horse. This poison, APTX (Apotoxin 4869), is experimental, and has never been used on humans before.

Instead of dying, Shinichi is wracked with pain and fever. It passes within a few hours, but leaves him looking like a six-year-old kid. The boy-genius detective is born!

See glossary

Roller Coaster Murder Case/
The Big Shrink
Shinichi Kudo
Ran Mori
APTX4869

See questions
2 28

Was Shinichi Kudo really a great detective?

Called the "Savior of the Police" for solving cases even the police have given up on, Shinichi Kudo is unquestionably one of the best detectives in Japan. But how could he be a master detective at the age of 17?

His calm and rational thinking comes from his father, and Shinichi draws on a storehouse of personal knowledge that includes an in-depth understanding of drugs, explosives, and medicine. Paired with his physical training and abilities that could have made him a professional soccer player, he is a total crime-fighting package. His self-reliance is even more important since civilians (even detectives) aren't allowed to carry weapons in Japan.

Shinichi does have a flair for the dramatic that often borders on arrogance. He commonly uses rather snobbish phrases when he explains a mystery, but since his skill more than backs it up, he garners more female fans with every

See glossary

Company President's Daughter Kidnapping Case/ Kidnapped Debutante The Flying Locked-Room! Shinichi Kudo's First Case

See questions
52

case.

Until he crosses paths with the Black
Organization, Shinichi has it all.

03 *Why did he choose the name Conan Edogawa?*

Forced to hide his identity in his new form, Shinichi assumes the name Conan Edogawa. The name comes as a split second decision when discovered in his house by his girlfriend, Ran Mori. By combining the name of his favorite author, Sir Arthur Conan Doyle, and Japan's most famous mystery writer, Rampo Edogawa, he declares himself Conan Edogawa. A strange name in Japan, for which he is often called a foreigner.

But why couldn't he tell Ran what happened? On Professor's Agasa's advice, Shinichi must hide his true identity to protect those he loves from the Black Organization. If they know he lives, he and anyone who knows what happened will be in grave danger.

Despite hiding in this new identity, Conan will use his instincts and skills to continue as a detective. His childlike appearance won't stop him from uncovering the Black Organization.

⑤ee glossary

Company President's Daughter Kidnapping Case/ Kidnapped Debutante
Holmes Freak Murder Case
Hiroshi Agasa

04 As a child again, how has Conan's life changed?

I If Conan ever hopes to return to his former self, he must learn the true identity of the Black Organization. Yet a child doesn't have the freedom he once had, and he can't attract too much attention to himself.

To all appearances, Prof. Agasa treats Conan as his own family. At the professor's urging, Ran and her family agree to let Conan live with them, believing that his parents are overseas. Luckily, Ran's father Kogoro is a private detective, though not a very good one. Proximity to a real detective makes Conan's work much easier to hide, despite Kogoro's reluctance to let a young kid hang around.

Ran likes having Conan around because she thinks he's cute and reminds her a bit of Shinichi somehow. Living so close with his girlfriend makes Conan nervous, but also gives him a chance to see how she really feels about Shinichi. When she tells him she loves Shinichi, it makes him realize how deeply he

cares for her as well.

There is a minor problem in this arrangement, though. He knew Kogoro wasn't the best detective around, but he never realized how little work he got because of it. Left with no other choice, Conan helps Kogoro solve cases (often without Kogoro realizing it) to boost the Mori Detective Agency's reputation and hopefully gain more contacts to investigate the Black Organization.

But how can Conan make Kogoro into a famous detective?

See glossary

Company President's Daughter Kidnapping Case/ Kidnapped Debutante
Kogoro Mori

05 How can Conan do detective work as a child?

Conan's deductive abilities are undiminished, and even most of his athletic technique remains, yet he looks like a little boy again. Prof. Agasa helps Conan make up for some of the physical shortcomings, like his invention of Kicking Power Reinforcement Shoes.

The largest problem is Conan's public perception. Should he solve crimes like he did as Shinichi, he'd cause a media frenzy as a prodigy child and surely attract the attention of the Black Organization. His only option is to help someone else solve each mystery, usually Kogoro. By tagging along to crime scenes with Kogoro, he finds the clues everyone else missed, and calls attention to them with cries of "What's that?!" or "Look at this!"

If all Conan's attempts fail, then he resorts to another invention of Prof. Agasa's: a watch with a hidden tranquilizer gun inside. His usual target is Kogoro, who ends up sleeping in a chair or leaning against a wall

while Conan solves the case. Conan uses a voice changer hidden within his bow tie, so everyone believes they are hearing Kogoro speak, not Conan. Word begins to spread, and Kogoro soon becomes known as "The Sleeping Kogoro," and the Mori Detective Agency's fame starts to spread.

See glossary

Watch Tranquilizer Gun
Bowtie Voice Changer
Magnified Kicking Power
Shoes

See questions
2 52

06 What kind of girl is Ran Mori?

Friends with Shinichi since kindergarten, Ran is also 17 years old. After the two of them got caught up in an incident in New York, her feelings for him grew stronger, and she began to wish for more than friendship. Shinichi cares deeply for her as well, but whenever they're together, they've never been able to share their true feelings for each other. Conan didn't know how serious she was about him until speaking with her after Shinichi's "disappearance."

To try and allay her fears for his safety, he tells her that Shinichi is on a difficult case, and will be gone for a while. She's accepted this story, but she still goes crazy if she suspects another woman getting close to Shinichi.

Everyone thinks Ran is just another pretty face. What most people don't realize is she's a master of karate, and can perform great feats of strength and agility, like jumping from a second story building and landing unharmed. Yet she is a young woman as well, taking

care of the housework for her father since her parents split up and afraid of ghosts and horror stories.

She treats Conan like a little brother, and thinks nothing of bathing with him in hot springs and such. Conan is reluctant, and terrified she'll beat him senseless when she finds out the truth.

Ran Mori is no ordinary name, either. She is named for Arsène Lupin creator Maurice LeBlanc.

ee glossary

Eri Kisaki

See questions
3 | 7 | 8 | 9 | 10

07 What kind of person is Kogoro Mori?

A former homicide detective, Kogoro Mori runs a private detective agency in Beikacho. Before Conan came, he spent more time betting on horses, drinking beer, and watching TV. To celebrate closing one of his rare cases 10 years ago, he spent more than he earned on a night partying and drinking. That was the last straw for his wife, who moved out soon after.

Kogoro really is a second-rate detective, as evidenced by his wildly inaccurate conclusions and ideas, yet he always manages to put everything together at the end (only because of Conan). Called "The Sleeping Kogoro" for his habit of solving cases while apparently unconscious, and "Kogoro Akechi of the Heisei Era" after one of Rampo Edogawa's main characters, he has recently risen to fame. Solving cases when he's asleep doesn't seem odd to him; he truly believes he solves them. Neither does he find it strange that he often doesn't remember cases or feels

See glossary

An Idol's Locked Room
Murder Case
Juzo Megure

19

sleepy around Conan. Oblivious or carefree, these peculiarities don't seem to bother him.

08 Is Kogoro Mori good at anything?

While he may seem like a failure as a detective, father and husband, Kogoro isn't a total loss. He has a cool head when it comes to even the worst situation, and can often determine the correct time of death with no coroner's input. Add expert marksmanship to the short list, and stories of him once being a skilled cop may just have some truth to them.

His understanding of human nature is greater than that of Conan or Heiji Hattori, in large part because of his life experiences. And though he may need Conan's assistance most of the time, he has been known to solve cases unaided.

Though never decorated with tournament awards or titles, Kogoro is a superior judo martial artist. Because he believes talent alone could do it all, his lack of practice and confidence during actual tournaments made winning impossible.

Maybe he isn't the greatest detective in the

See glossary

Kogoro's Class Reunion Murder Case
The Memories of First Love Case
Heiji Hattori

See questions
7 9 10

world, but it's hard to not like him.

E ri Kisaki, Ran's mother and Kogoro's wife, is a star lawyer only a year younger than Kogoro. For the last ten years she's been separated from him and goes by her maiden name even though they are not officially divorced.

Like Shinichi and Ran, Eri and Kogoro were childhood friends, only their friends said they would never last as a couple. Quiet, beautiful, and studious in school, Eri was a polar opposite of the mischievous and not-so-handsome Kogoro. In fact, Eri and Yukiko, Shinichi's mother, tied for first place in a high school beauty contest.

Eri passed the most difficult entrance exam in the nation to be accepted to Tokyo University and went on to easily pass the Japanese Bar exam. Now she's known as the "Queen of Justice" for both winning countless impossible cases and as a play on her last name ("Kisaki" is queen in Japanese). Her last name is also a tribute to American mystery

writer Ellery Queen.

No one understands why she married Kogoro.

Eri is one of the more skilled characters of the series, so much so that when she explains a current case to Yukiko, Conan remarks that he has nothing to do, "these two will do it all by themselves." This may also be indicative of Conan's perception of Eri; he doesn't like her much. Years before when he was growing up, he only remembers her yelling at him.

See glossary

Yukiko Kudo
Coffee Shop Murder Case

See questions
10

Will Kogoro and Eri ever get back together?

Eri counts only two good things to come of her marriage with Kogoro: her daughter Ran, and that she learned how to perform judo throws. Unhappy with her marriage, she even warns Ran against marrying childhood friends and detectives. And with Kogoro acting silly and sentimental around women, including Eri, the two constantly fight, no matter what their daughter might hope for.

Despite all this, they don't hate each other, and even seem to care for each other in their own way. Eri keeps a cat named Goro, even if Kogoro still hasn't figured out it's named after him. And Kogoro acts stubborn, but he bends over backward to make her happy. When her ring went missing, he searched for it. When he met Eri's favorite baseball player, he begged for an autographed ball to give her.

Once he asked her to come back to him and said that he couldn't take not having her there, but she pretended not to hear. Yet even

now, she listens to his words (she recorded him when he said it), smiling to herself while telling herself she still won't forgive him.

Looking back when Ran and Shinichi were in first grade, Eri and Kogoro were very much in love. With such a deep connection, reconciliation is always possible.

See glossary

Shinichi Kudo's Childhood Adventure
Scuba Diving Murder Case
Kogoro Mori

See questions
7 8 9

11 *Just who is Professor Agasa?*

Professor Agasa lives next door to Shinichi and is an inventor in his 50s. He is the first to learn of Conan's true identity. At first thinking it was a childish prank, he dismissed it. This was until Conan told the professor confidential information only Shinichi knew, and deduced the professor's visit to the restaurant Columbo earlier that day.

Conan refers to Prof. Agasa's inventions as junk, but he knows them for the ingenious things they are. In fact, the professor makes quite a lot of money from his patents and the big businesses that use them. He created Conan's Voice-Changing Bow Tie, Super Sneakers, and many more gadgets that allow Conan to get the job done.

When Conan isn't at school, he and his friends Ayumi, Mitsuhiko and Genta like visiting the professor and often ride in his Volkswagen Beetle to soccer games and other trips. As these trips often turn into a mystery

to be solved, the professor helps where he can, even to the point of creating the illusion of adults speaking in time to Conan's Voice-Changer.

Prof. Agasa is single, overweight and completely bald. He still thinks of his first love, Fusae Campbell Kinoshita, from back in 6th grade. She's now president of a major fashion company. They meet for the first time in 40 years. Will his love be returned?

See glossary

Genta Kojima
Ayumi Yoshida
Mitsuhiko Tsuburaya

See questions
47 56 57

12 Who are Ran's other friends?

Sonoko Suzuki is the daughter of one of the richest men in Japan, and another childhood friend of both Ran and Shinichi. Even though she's from a distinguished family, Sonoko is down to earth and very normal, though very opinionated at times.

She often teases Ran about her relationship with Shinichi, trying to get Ran to be honest with herself and her feelings for Shinichi. She even took a picture of Ran in her swimsuit on a trip to the beach and sent the picture to Shinichi to see what she could stir up. Simple and direct, she only has the best of intentions for her friends.

Unwittingly, she sometimes helps without even realizing. A few times she's become the master detective, falling to Conan's tranquilizer in times of need to solve the case. Like Kogoro, she's largely unaware of being manipulated, and some call her "The Sleeping Sonoko."

Ran also became friends with Kazuha Toyama, Heiji Hattori's girlfriend. After getting over the initial suspicion of Ran trying to steal her boyfriend, Ran and Kazuha are great friends.

See glossary

Sonoko Suzuki
Kazuha Toyama

See questions
5

13 Does Sonoko have a boyfriend?

Sonoko teases Ran about her relationship with Shinichi partly because she dreams of finding love and can't wait to have a true boyfriend. Her quest to find that boyfriend leads to antics and trouble throughout the series.

She seems indiscriminate at first in her attempts to get Ran to go pick up boys with her, but it actually ends up showing how high her standards really are, because none of the boys they find measure up. One nearly kills her, but another saves her from imminent danger.

His name is Makoto Kyogoku, a strong high school boy, and he ends up falling head over heels in love with Sonoko. Captain of the Karate team at their high school, he is completely smitten with Sonoko after seeing her at one of Ran's karate matches. He always seems to know when she is in danger and does everything he can to save her, no matter where he is or what he's doing. Seeing

Sonoko dressed in revealing clothes brings out his conservative side, and no matter what the situation, he says and hears the most obvious meaning possible. When he gets a message from Sonoko saying she's knitting a sweater for someone she likes, he thinks she's making it for another man.

See glossary

Makoto Kyogoku

Can't Ran tell who Conan really is?

No matter how well Conan plays the child, he can't disguise his intellect and skills forever. Ran doesn't quickly notice these things, but even she's starting to suspect there's more going on with this boy. Mannerisms and expressions unique to Shinichi leak through from time to time, and after seeing Conan without his glasses, Ran sees the resemblance to Shinichi at that age.

Still, without a plausible explanation for how Conan could be Shinichi, believing her suspicions is difficult at best. But doubt casts enough of a shadow for her to put an end to things like bathing together. She nearly confronts Conan with her suspicions, but is dissuaded by a phone call from Prof. Agasa masquerading as someone else via a voice-changer.

It can't be long before she puts all the pieces together, especially since they live in such proximity to each other.

Further proof comes when Conan is shot by

a bank robber and in desperate need of a blood transfusion. No one knows his blood type, but Ran declares that her blood type is the same and that they should use hers. She bases this on Shinichi's blood type, and the incident almost makes Conan tell her everything.

Instead, he and Ai Haibara come up with an experimental antidote to the poison that turned him into a child, though it only lasts for a few days. Ai pretends to be Conan so he and Shinichi can be seen in the same room together, hopefully putting to rest all ideas that he is Conan. This quells Ran's theories, though they still lurk somewhere deep in her mind.

A third event causes the issue to come up again. This is when Ran discovers that a text message she'd sent to Shinichi has ended up on Conan's cell phone. Still convinced from Conan and Ai's charade, she quickly believes Conan when he tells her that Shinichi contacts him on a daily basis. This does mean, however, that Shinichi had to give out his email address and cell phone number, and now constantly gets calls from Ran even while he's with her.

It's only a matter of time before she'll find out the truth.

15 *Is there any detective better than Conan?*

Among all the famous detectives that appear in Case Closed, Conan continues to prove that he is in a league above them all. Even in showdowns between the most well known detectives, Conan obliterates the competition.

In the "Detective Koshien," a high school student competition, only Conan and Heiji Hattori find the real culprit. In battles with the Phantom Thief Kid, an equal to Heiji, Conan isn't able to catch Kid, but stops his announced plans every time. While Heiji is close to Conan in skill, he still falls short and Conan proves himself again and again.

So is no one better than Conan? Not quite. There is one person Conan has never bested.

Yusaku Kudo, Conan's father.

As a famous mystery writer, his most acclaimed and bestselling work is the Night Baron series. He owns a home in both Beikacho and Los Angeles, but flies all around the world with his wife avoiding editors after

his manuscripts.

It comes as no surprise that Yusaku's abilities and fame have influenced Shinichi. As a child he read both his father's novels and the classics, then moved on to solving his own mysteries in middle school with a bit of help from his father.

Immediately after Shinichi's poisoning, his father senses something is terribly wrong. He assumes the Night Baron character to warn and tease Shinichi. No matter how much Shinichi accomplishes as a detective, his father still toys with him.

Until Shinichi can outsmart his father, he knows he will never be the greatest detective in the world. It's a long road, but he will find a way.

See glossary

Conan Edogawa Kidnapping Case
The Gathered Detectives! Shinichi Kudo vs. Phantom Thief Kid
Three Days with Heiji Hattori (2)
Phantom Thief Kid
Yusaku Kudo

See questions
43 44

16 *How did Conan get so good at impersonations?*

C onan is making a career out of impersonations, whether he's pretending to be Kogoro delivering the case-breaking explanation, or simply playing the little boy he appears to be. For another caught in the same situation, Ai Haibara refuses to play the child, and instead behaves more like her true age. She also considers Conan to be quite the actor.

Gadgets alone don't do it all for him; so where does this talent come from?

Conan has his mother to thank for his chameleon skills, for she was once an actress known the world over. When she played a part in one of Yusaku's mystery dramas, she fell in love and soon announced her retirement, choosing to marry and make her life with him. Yukiko quickly distanced herself from her fame, but her talent remained. With an amazing sense for human nature, and able to speak fluently in all of Japan's regional dialects, English, and other languages, her

talents have been passed on to her son with little formal training. By studying as an apprentice under the great magician Touichi Kuroba, the original Phantom Thief Kid, she perfected the art of disguise as well.

Her talent and skill are put to the test in the events surrounding the encounter with Vermouth, a power-player in the Black Organization.

See glossary

First Phantom Thief Kid
Sharon Vineyard

See questions
32 44

17 How does Conan deal with elementary school the second time around?

Since Conan appears to be 6 years old, he must behave as a little boy, and that means going to elementary school even though he already knows how to read, write and do all the things high schoolers are taught. He's found good friends at school who help him overcome the annoyances of studying things he already knows.

Three stand out above all others: the self-proclaimed leader Genta Kojima, cool and composed Mitsuhiko Tsubaraya, and cute little Ayumi Yoshida. The later addition of Ai Haibara to the group creates the Junior Detective League.

Heavy, not so bright, and generally simplistic, Genta follows the model of leaders in traditional boy's comics. And when trouble comes around, Conan usually takes the lead anyway, so Genta's position is really just for show most of the time.

Mitsuhiko at first seems to be nothing more than the quiet brainy kid, but soon

proves that he possesses a deep understanding and insight far beyond anything children his age are supposed to have. While he can't always keep up with Conan and Ai, it seems he really is a child prodigy, given that his age is true, while Conan and Ai have many more years of experience. In fact, Mitsuhiko could even be seen as a younger version of Shinichi, with a very promising future ahead of him. Apparently, even the author's perception of his character changed for the better after hearing Mitsuhiko's voice actor in the anime series.

Until Ai joined the Junior Detective League, Ayumi was the only girl in the group. Quiet and cute, she loves animals and is very soft-spoken. After sensing Ai's maturity, she only allows herself to call her Miss Haibara, and seems to understand a great deal more about human relations than she ever lets on.

See glossary

The Haunted House Case

See questions
18 19

With the exception of Conan and Ai, all members of the Junior Detective league are actually their apparent age, but it seems that exposure to these two brings out extraordinary abilities in these children.

Genta, while a bit slow, has a gift for remembering details. He may not understand everything he sees, but details he provides often help solve the case. With only a glance, he can later recount not only a full description of the suspect, but a complete description of the environment around him at that time, down to the smallest point.

Ayumi's greatest asset is her childlike imagination and manner. Conan must work to act the part of the child when pointing out clues, but for Ayumi it comes naturally. She fully understands the significance of little pieces of evidence and always wraps it in the easy innocence of a child's words.

The Junior Detective League is really

giving Mitsuhiko the chance to grow and shine in his own way. He is a storehouse of knowledge, and tends to take Conan's place when he isn't around. The longer he's in the League, the more confident he becomes. The bravery he now shows in helping his friends would've been unheard of in the beginning of the series.

Originally just an annoyance to Conan, the members of the Junior Detective League are turning into a true team. In no time at all, they've all become real detectives.

See glossary

Ayumi kidnapping case
Mushrooms, Bears, and the Junior Detective League
Genta's Misfortune
Mitsuhiko in the Forest of Indecision
Find the Mark on the Butt!

See questions
17 19

The Junior Detective League and love?

They may be children, but even their romantic and everyday connections are quite complex.

Genta and Mitsuhiko have always liked Ayumi, but she's quickly fallen for the smart, active Conan, who is the "same age" as her. She believes she and Conan are destined for each other.

Ai's presence in the group is another thing entirely. Her grownup airs at first make the boys nervous, but Mitsuhiko soon finds himself enthralled by her. Conan has tried to discourage him from liking her, but Mitsuhiko can't give up.

On the other hand, Ai seems to trust Conan very much, even more because they're both in the same situation. They always watch out for each other, but sometimes she flirts with him. Even Shinichi's mother has noticed this behavior, mentioning to him that Ai's always watching him. Could it be genuine though? Ai makes a habit of concealing her true feelings,

See glossary

Ayumi Kidnapping Case
Mushrooms, Bears, and the Junior Detective League

See questions
18 19

so perhaps this is for another reason. Ai knows Conan is committed to Ran, whom Ai sees almost like a sister. How does Ai really feel about Conan?

Wearing a white lab coat far too large for her, Ai Haibara was found collapsed on Shinichi's doorstep, and now lives with Prof. Agasa. Like Conan, she looks like a child, but seems even more mature than Conan. Who is she really?

Her real name is Shiho Miyano, code name Sherry, and she was the scientist who created APTX 4869, the poison that changed Shinichi into Conan. After her parents died when she was very young, the Black Organization became the only family she and her older sister Akemi had.

This all changed when the Black Organization murdered Akemi. Shocked, Shiho demanded answers, and when they refused, she halted research on APTX 4869. Rather than give in to her demands, the Black Organization imprisoned her for betrayal. Certain they would kill her, Shiho tried to end her life by taking the experimental drug. As with Conan, she instead became a child again

and was able to escape the Black Organization, She subsequently sought out Shinichi Kudo.

Shrinking to child-like size didn't come as a complete surprise to her, for she'd witnessed the same effect in some animals during the testing phase of the drug. When the Black Organization searched the Kudo home for signs that Shinichi was still alive, she had quietly noted that his children's clothes had gone, leading her to believe that he may have survived in a smaller form.

The name Ai Haibara was given to her by Prof. Agasa, inspired by Cordelia Gray (Gray = Hai) and V. I Wachowski (I = Ai). He wanted her to write Ai with the character for love, but Shiho insisted that it be written with the character for loneliness.

Now, she lives the life of an elementary student while researching day and night for a way to reverse the effects of APTX 4869.

See glossary

The Girl from the Black Organization
One Billion Yen Robbery Case
Akemi Miyano

See questions
21 28 10 37 38

Chapter 02

Battling the Black Organization

21 | *Could Ai actually be a spy?*

A i is cold by nature and therefore could be a spy. But it is highly unlikely.

A scientist like her father was, Ai grew up in the United States with her sister. Her pride is what keeps her from behaving like a child again, and instead she is sarcastic and makes no effort to hide her intelligence. She appears indifferent to most events, but seems to care for Ayumi like a little sister.

Though Ai usually gets caught up in incidents with Conan and helping him with her brains and scientific knowledge, she has little patience for being a "detective freak." She and Heiji Hattori are some of Conan's staunchest allies. She is also often Conan's voice of reason, restraining him from extreme lengths he may consider to solve a case.

Ai's perception of Ran is a shifting one, for on one hand she feels guilty for indirectly causing Shinichi to shrink to child-size again as a result of her drug. On the other hand,

she wonders if she'll end up as Ran's rival, competing for Shinichi's attentions.

Since she spent most of her life in the Black Organization, she knows its inner workings very well, and knows just how dangerous it can be. She can easily spot anyone who is a part of the Black Organization, and their mere presence is enough to agitate the normally calm Ai. What exactly is the relationship between her and an important Black Organization member known only as Gin?

See glossary

Atsushi Miyano
Elena Miyano
Akemi Miyano
Gin

See questions
19 28 37

Does Conan have any rivals?

Conan may be "Shinichi Kudo of the East," but there is another high school detective known as "Heiji Hattori of the West."

The son of Osaka's Chief Commissioner, Heiji has seen many cases from a very young age. When it comes to Shinichi, Heiji's competitive streak comes out, and he even journeys to Tokyo to meet his rival and challenge him. Conan uses the temporary antidote to return to his normal self during Heiji's visit, and finds the truth after Heiji falls for the culprit's false clues. He admits defeat and returns home to Osaka.

In their next encounter, Heiji discovers Conan's true identity, but agrees to keep it secret. Afterwards, they work on more and more cases together, and end up very good friends. This secret is getting harder to keep each day though, as Heiji, the more hot-blooded and passionate of the two, often forgets and calls Conan by his real last name

See glossary

Diplomat Murder Case
Heizo Hattori
Baijiu

See questions
23 54

Kudo, even in front of Ran and Kogoro.

Heiji is a kendo master and learned from the best instructors in the country. Few people his age can match him in a kendo match.

J ust like Ran and Shinichi, Heiji and his girlfriend Kazuha Toyama grew up together, and her father works for his father as a commissioner. She's cute, usually wears her hair in a ponytail, and is a 2nd degree black belt in Aikido.

Also like Shinichi and Ran, the two of them aren't really officially dating, as they have trouble telling each other how they really feel. It's clear that Kazuha really likes Heiji, but his trips to Tokyo to meet Conan make her wonder if he has a girl there and is keeping it secret. For a while she thought Ran was the girl, but they've since overcome that misunderstanding.

Their relationship is at a standstill, despite everything. It's not that Heiji doesn't care for Kazuha, but more because he's a bit clueless when it comes to dealing with girls, and always wrapped up in being a detective. He doesn't even completely understand his own feelings, as evidenced by not knowing why it

bothers him to see Kazuha really getting along with another guy.

Heiji tries, but when distracted by a case, he forgets about everything else, even a date with Kazuha. Until he's over the "detective bug," Kazuha's troubles will never end.

🆂ee glossary

Toyama

Nearly all the cases in the series occur in Tokyo. Here, the police department is divided into two groups: the Metropolitan Police Department with jurisdiction over greater Tokyo, and Section 1, a specialized unit of the MPD that handles particularly heinous crimes. Section 1 has the best policemen, although as Kogoro used to work there, perhaps they not all the cream of the crop. Regardless, Conan usually works with Section 1, helping out as a detective.

Let's meet some of the key officers of the MPD's Section 1.

Juzo Megure [Inspector]

Seen in a trench coat all year round. He wears his hat to bed, which is said to be a result of an incident while he was a rookie. Kogoro used to report to him, and all the members of the Section 1 3rd Investigation Team still do.

Kogoro still treats him like his boss at times, and never feels he quite measures up to him.

Wataru Takagi [Sergeant]

Originally, Wataru was only around to explain a crime scene to other characters, but his sarcastic manner has become so popular with Conan fans that he makes more regular appearances in the story than ever before.

Wataru is well-meaning, but often makes mistakes and incorrect assumptions due to his age and lack of experience. Lt. Sato calls him soft-hearted and clumsy, and she worries for him. In times of crisis, his bravery awakens and he's willing to risk his own life to save others.

His crush on Lt. Sato eventually leads to the beginning of their relationship, and the two grow very close when investigating a case involving her late father.

For Conan, his personality is a bit disarming, and he often forgets to play the child when around Wataru.

Miwako Sato [Lieutenant]

Lt. Sato is considered a model police officer, with good looks and a bright, frank personality. She looks after Wataru like a younger brother before she starts to appreciate his dependability and other qualities, and now the two are deeply in love with each other.

In working with Conan, she recognizes his abilities, to the point that Conan fears she'll find him out sooner or later. If she's on a case, he tries to avoid some of his usual tricks, like the "Sleeping Kogoro" act, for fear of being found out.

Ninzaburo Shiratori [Inspector]

A career police officer, Ninzaburo passed the Public Servant Type 1 exam at an early age, almost guaranteeing his future as a successful member of the police department. Before Sato and Takagi became a couple, Ninzaburo dated Sato, but it ended abruptly when Takagi got in the way. He still harbors feelings for Sato, and tries to ruin their relationship, even to the point of sending a stakeout team after them while on a date under the pretense of breaking up a drug deal.

Officer Chiba

A coworker of Takagi and a huge fan of anime and blockbuster movies, he spends his off-duty time glued to the TV. This makes him a bit overweight because he's a big eater and gets very little exercise.

Officer Yumi

Though she's a traffic officer, she's usually the go-between for Takagi and Sato. She loves her two dogs Suta and Hachi, possibly named after Starsky and Hutch.

See glossary
Megure's Secret

See questions
25 55

The mutual attraction between Miwako Sato and Wataru Takagi develops slowly but surely. But just as things are getting serious, Officer Sato tells Officer Takagi that it would be better if the two of them remained merely friends. As things seem to be going so well, a baffled Takagi asks for an explanation.

Sato tells him that the men in her life tend to meet with violent ends: her father was murdered, and the man she loved three years previous also died in the line of duty. Sato's fear of losing the ones she loves has grown so intense in the meantime that she can't allow herself to love Takagi, in case the worst happens again.

The incident in question three years previous involved Jinpei Matsuda. Like Sato, he was a young officer in MPD Section 1 before Takagi was assigned to the department. Though he only ended up serving for a week, it was enough time for he and Sato to grow

close.

Matsuda's particular specialty was bomb disposal, and on his seventh day of service, he went out to investigate a bomb threat. He succeeded in defusing the bomb, only to encounter a nasty surprise — the bomb was hiding a second explosive with a three-second timer, which only revealed itself once the first bomb had been deactivated. Unable to defuse the second device in time, Matsuda was killed.

Three years later, the criminal responsible for Matsuda's death strikes again, and Takagi rises to the challenge. With the help of Conan and the Junior Detective League, Takagi successfully eliminates the first bomb while deducing the presence of the second bomb, defusing it as well.

Proving himself a survivor to Sato, she welcomes him back into her life and continues to pray for his safety as her true love.

See glossary

Metropolitan Police Detective Love Story
The Trembling MPD: Twelve Million Hostages
Jinpei Matsuda

26 Who assists Conan when he's working outside of Tokyo?

T he Metropolitan Police Department has jurisdiction over the capital, but the National Police Agency handles all cases outside of Tokyo. When Conan or Kogoro are working out of town, they're partnered with local law enforcement from prefectural police departments. Like the MPD, the local police are often stymied by the strange suspects Conan and Kogoro run up against. Their police work is sometimes questionable, but Conan never fails to back them up no matter where the crime occurs.

Inspector Sango Yokomizo

He first appears as a member of the Saitama Prefectural Police, but later transfers to Kanagawa. Has a gentle demeanor, but not much skill as a policeman. After seeing Kogoro's detective work, or rather Conan's detective work masquerading as Kogoro's, he greatly respects Kogoro and trusts him implicitly.

Inspector Jugo Yokomizo

Twin brother to Sango Yokomizo, but a polar opposite in personality. He works out of the Shizuoka precinct, and is as rough with suspects and civilians alike as his brother is gentle. Under normal circumstances, he would never agree to work a case with his brother, but there is one exceptional instance where he cooperates with Sango in secret.

Officer Misao Yamamura

Whenever Conan and Kogoro find themselves in Gunma, this hapless officer is seemingly always along for the ride. His inability to do anything without Conan's help makes people wonder how he ever became a policeman, but he sticks with the job and never fails to appear in Gunma to lend his assistance. The frequency of his appearances was never intended, but once the author heard Japanese voice actor Toshio Furukawa's comedic performance as Yamamura, he asked to see more of the character.

I   t's currently unclear whether Conan and Ai can ever regain their adult selves, but there is one possibility: a type of Chinese wine called Baijiu.

Conan first samples Baijiu when fellow high school detective Heiji Hattori, his rival from the West, offers it to the Mori Detective Agency as a gift. It has a high alcohol content of 35% proof, but in the feverish state Conan is in at the time, he unquestioningly accepts it as medicine. With a cold already raging in his system, the strong liquor has a powerful effect on Conan's child body and he develops intense dizzy spells. While investigating a murder at the embassy with Kogoro and Hattori, his fever peaks and he collapses.

It is then that the astonishing effects of Baijiu first become known: the combination of the virus in Conan's system and some property of the wine react in a way that temporarily nullifies the effects of APTX4869. As a result, Conan is able to return to his life as Detective

Shinichi Kudo for a short time. He solves cases with aplomb, wins out over his rival Hattori, and is all too be briefly reunited with Ran.

Some time later, when Ai Haibara's life is in danger from a member of the Black Organization, Conan suggests she try drinking Baijiu. By returning to her 18-year-old body for a few hours, she is able to slip under the Black Organization's noses and escape danger.

The common factor in both circumstances is that Conan and Ai are sick with colds when they drink the Baijiu. The specific properties of the Chinese wine that counteract the APTX4869 are unknown, but it can only be used in this way once before the chemical develops a resistance to it. Because of this, Baijiu is not a permanent cure for their condition, but Ai continues to study the strange wine in order to perfect a true antidote.

See glossary

Reuniting with the Black Organization
Pisco

See questions
14

T he greatest mystery in Case Closed is the nature and makeup of the Black Organization, a longtime enemy of both Conan and Haibara. Initially, the only observable fact about the group is that it is an organized crime syndicate whose operations span the globe. Beyond that, almost nothing is known — the size of its membership, the location of its headquarters, and even its official name are mysteries to this day. Thanks to Conan and Haibara's efforts, however, a few facts have come to light.

First, the Black Organization's scope is considerable, and it is active in a wide variety of criminal enterprises. From drug trafficking to more hi-tech ventures such as data hacking, there's little the Black Organization won't stoop to.

Though it's impossible to say how many members the organization has, so far Conan and Haibara have encountered fewer than 20, each of them unique in some way. To preserve

the organization's secrecy, its members are strict about using code names relating to alcohol, such as "Gin" or "Vodka."

Whatever it is, the Black Organization has amply demonstrated its shocking commitment to complete its missions by any means necessary. It has no qualms about killing its own members should they become a liability, and it won't hesitate to murder as many innocent bystanders as it has to. Its methods are both unpredictable and meticulously planned, such as in the incident where it plans a bomb attack on a bullet train.

See glossary

That Person
Gin
Vodka
Vermouth
Calvados
Pisco
Sherry

See questions
35

29 | Who is the Black Organization's main operative?

The Black Organization's central figure seems to be a man code-named "Gin." Like most facts about the organization, his real name, age, and nationality are unknown. He drives a Porsche 356A, carries a Beretta M1934, and is a heavy smoker. To Conan's mind, Gin represents the entire Black Organization.

He never shows signs of agitation or panic, remaining calm at all times, even when about to kill. His steady hand makes him a first-rate marksman. He tries to kill Shinichi Kudo by forcing him to take APTX4869, and he is also the one who murders Akemi Miyano, Ai Haibara's sister.

He and Ai were deeply involved at one point. He was once able to identify a strand of hair from Shiho Miyano (Haibara's adult self) on sight, and according to Vermouth, the two of them were sexually involved. Now, however, when Ai senses Gin's presence, her terror of the man causes her to shudder

uncontrollably.

Being a hit man, he is naturally prudent, but his casual disregard for human life means he usually forgets the faces of those he has killed. His inability to remember Shinichi Kudo's face is the only thing preventing him from identifying Conan and finishing the job he started.

Gin also has a right-hand man, code named Vodka, who works directly under Gin and refers to him as "Brother." He was with Gin when the two of them blackmailed Shinichi Kudo and administered the APTX4869. Unlike the tall, slender Gin, Vodka is powerfully built and is never seen without his sunglasses.

Vodka is a master of disguise and assists Gin in whatever ways necessary. His carelessness is usually his undoing, as when he throws away a cigarette with traces of his saliva on it, or fires a gun with police nearby. His inattentiveness earns him constant reprimands from Gin.

See glossary

Gin
Vodka
Vermouth

See questions
4

The influence of Black Organization is mostly hidden, but every so often something happens to highlight its presence in society. One such incident involves Kenzo Masuyama, owner of a car maker and secret executive member of the Black Organization under the name "Pisco."

Pisco owes his success to his allegiance and contributions to the organization, and he enjoys a status within the syndicate equal to Gin. His deadly accurate marksmanship further indicates that behind the law-abiding façade lies a bloody past uncharacteristic of such a successful businessman.

The incident in question comes about when Pisco is hired to assassinate Shigehiko Nomiguchi, a politician and low-ranking member of the organization, at a memorial benefit for Akira Sakamaki. As soon as the lights dim for a slideshow, Pisco shoots the chandelier, bringing it down on Nomiguchi's head.

Believing the operation to have gone off without a hitch, Pisco quietly slips out, but complications arise when he meets Ai Haibara on the way out and recognizes her as Shiho Miyano. (Pisco had previously been close to Haibara's parents, and referred to Ai as "Little Shiho.") With Vermouth's help, he imprisons her in the hotel wine cellar, but their plan fails as a result of Conan's intervention.

Pisco's luck worsens when it turns out his getaway isn't as clean as he thought and he is accidentally photographed on the scene. When the photo runs in the next day's newspaper, Gin receives orders from "that person" to eliminate Pisco.

The example of Kenzo Masuyama and Shigehiko Nomiguchi shows how the Black Organization has its tendrils sunk deep into financial and political circles, which fuel its expansion to its current global scope.

See glossary

Reuniting with the Black Organization
Pisco

See questions
35

31 What is Jodie Saintemillion's secret?

Jodie Saintemillion, a beautiful 28-year-old English teacher, has recently joined the staff of Teitan High School. She claims to have come to Japan as a hardcore video gamer seeking to live in the country where all the best games are made, but there's evidence that her real agenda is something entirely different.

For one thing, photos of Ran and Conan are taped to her bathroom sink, and for another, she pretends to speak clumsy Japanese even though she is perfectly fluent. Most mysterious of all is her oft-stated motto, "A secret makes a woman a woman," something that a very different woman has also been known to say.

That woman is Vermouth, a female operative of the Black Organization. Her public identity is Chris Vineyard, a famous Hollywood actress, like her mother Sharon Vineyard. If Vermouth and Jodie are indeed one and the same, some questions still need addressing: why infiltrate Teitan High rather

than Teitan Elementary School, where Conan attends? Why protect Conan and Ran when they were accidentally involved in a bus hijacking?

One thing's certain: there are still many questions about Jodie Saintemillion. But there are also many clues. We won't reveal what they are here, but keep an eye on her during the middle of the Case Closed story for some exciting revelations.

ee glossary

Head On Battle with the Black Organization: Two Mysteries Beneath the Full Moon
Jodie Saintemillion

See questions
33 35

Is Sharon Vineyard connected to Conan or Ran?

C hris Vineyard is the public identity of Vermouth, a female operative of the Black Organization. But what of her mother Sharon? Apart from her Oscar-winning career as a Hollywood actress, she has some noteworthy connections to the main characters of the story.

Sharon is an old friend of Yukiko Kudo, Shinichi/Conan's mother. Yukiko and Sharon were both struggling actresses in their youth, and both apprenticed themselves to the stage magician Touichi Kuroba in order to learn his methods of disguise.

It may have been as a result of this family connection that Sharon met Shinichi Kudo and Ran Mori a year before the Case Closed story begins, in an episode that ran in Volume 35. At the time of the episode, Shinichi and Ran had just entered high school and are visiting Shinichi's parents in New York. Yukiko introduces Sharon to them as "my best friend."

Sharon tells the two teenagers about

her life, and how both her parents died in a fire shortly after her big-screen debut. Further tragedy followed when her husband succumbed to a terminal illness the day after she won her Academy Award. She also speaks of her daughter Chris, who followed in her footsteps as an actress but didn't have the "Vineyard talent." She is said to have died soon after, though neither Shinichi nor Ran knows the circumstances of her death.

Another important character also meets Shinichi and Ran during their stay in New York, and that character's actions and dialogue are clues to an important aspect of the overall Case Closed story. The reader/viewer is encouraged to pay special attention during that scene and consider what it might be hinting at.

See glossary

Shinichi Kudo N.Y. (New York) Case

See questions
16 31

Vermouth of the Black Organization has an uncanny talent for disguising herself as others, widely thought to have been learned from her mother Sharon. She may even now be disguised as someone close to Conan or Ran.

Of all the mysterious characters in Case Closed, she is the most enigmatic. One of her goals is to find Sherry, a traitor to the syndicate. Her mission is a success when she discovers that Sherry has been turned into a child, along with Shinichi Kudo. However, even when she learns this, she does nothing to report her findings to her superiors within the Black Organization. Instead, she works with a syndicate sniper called Calvados to assassinate Sherry, acting independently of the leaders of the Black Organization. Throughout it all, her motives remain unclear.

There are many other contradictions regarding Vermouth. She is a favorite of Gin and "that person" for her skills as an operative,

but she also has many enemies within the syndicate. She was once Gin's lover, but now claims that he "makes her sick." During her operation with Calvados, it becomes clear that he harbored feelings for the beautiful spy, but after his death it seems that she regarded him as little more than a pawn.

See glossary

That Person

See questions
29 37

T he one man whom the Black Organization considers its greatest enemy is Shuichi Akai, a legendary Japanese FBI agent nicknamed the Silver Bullet. "That person" watches Akai carefully, believing him to be the only man on earth capable of destroying the syndicate. Vermouth, on the other hand, has a very different opinion of Akai. Judging by her comments, it seems that she has hopes that Akai will succeed in breaking up the Black Organization for good.

As for Conan, it appears that Vermouth has similar hopes for him. Though she makes a cold-blooded attempt on Ai Haibara's life, she never raises a hand against Conan despite knowing his true identity as Shinichi Kudo. It's possible that she believes Conan could be a contingency plan in case the Silver Bullet fails.

The reason she'd want either Akai or Conan to succeed in bringing down the very organization she holds to be so dear has not been revealed. Perhaps she holds a grudge

against "that person," or perhaps she aims to take his place as the mastermind. One clue is that her body apparently holds some sort of secret related to the Black Organization's primary goal, which may be related to the Final Objective. Whatever her motives, Vermouth will definitely be a key player in the final chapters of the story.

S ee glossary

Shuichi Akai

See questions
28 37

Isn't anyone doing anything about the Black Organization?

Though the Black Organization is a global criminal organization, its members are careful never to leave any evidence of their crimes. Neither Tokyo's MPD nor Japan's NPA are aware of their existence, which is one reason Conan and Ai have to work so hard. International enforcement organizations such as the FBI and CIA, however, have been tracking the Black Organization for years.

One of the FBI agents dedicated to pursuing the Black Organization is Akai, the Silver Bullet who has already been mentioned. Other than him, there's Agent Jodie Starling, who has a personal reason for her war on the syndicate; Andre Camel, one of the best drivers alive, and a calm British native named James Black who directs their operations.

Less is known about the CIA's actions against the Black Organization, due to the high level of secrecy the organization maintains. However, it is certain that the CIA does have

agents investigating the syndicate, though their methods are very different to those of the FBI. Some CIA agents have even gone undercover as Black Organization members. Conan is not currently working with the CIA, but as his battle with the syndicate heats up, it's possible that he'll find himself fighting alongside them.

See glossary

Jodie Starling
Shinichi Akai
James Black
Hdemi Hondou
Ethan Hondou

See questions				
31	38	39	40	41
42				

36 Who is the leader of the Black Organization?

bsolutely nothing is known about the person who commands the Black Organization and its members. It may be a man or a woman, young or old, Asian or Westerner — not a single detail has come to light yet. Even Gin and Vermouth, senior syndicate members, refer to the leader only as "that person."

The only hint given so far is the leader's email address. Known only to a select few within the Black Organization, such as Vermouth, the email address plays a famous Japanese melody called "Nanatsu no Ko," or "The Seventh Child." According to Aoyama, the author, the name of "that person" has already appeared in the manga in some form.

It logically follows that the leader is someone readers are familiar with, so this hint has led to frantic fan speculation. Fan sites are abuzz with comments such as "Maybe it's Professor Agasa!" or "It has to be Kogoro Mori!" Some theories are well-founded and compelling, while

others are clearly crackpot suggestions meant only as jokes. However, any of them could still be true, until the author reveals the secret. The only other hint Aoyama has given so far is that "It's someone that Haibara would never have expected."

Aoyama also suggests that the true name of the syndicate, which has also never been revealed, is tied to the identity of its leader. If the Black Organization's real name were revealed, everyone would know who its leader is. This may turn out to be the biggest hint of all.

Whatever the secret is, once it's revealed, the Case Closed story will begin its final chapters. As a result, it may be some time before we find out who the mysterious leader really is...giving us all plenty of time to keep speculating.

See glossary
"that person."
Hiroshi Agasa

The syndicate's ultimate goal, like so much else about the organization, is still shrouded in mystery. A few clues can be had by observing its actions in general: we know it's put a lot of effort into developing new drugs and computer viruses, but it's hard to see the link between all of that. Yet all of the syndicate's activities are connected by a common thread, leading into its "Final Objective."

Vermouth says of the Black Organization that they "strive to become gods as well as devils...to go against the flow of time...and revive the dead." Some wonder if this means that the syndicate is researching methods of resurrection. However, this is refuted by former syndicate scientist Ai Haibara, who said, "Don't worry... my research had nothing to do with creating a dream drug like that." A better idea of the Black Organization's true aims might lie in her statement that "Most people on Earth would be incapable of.

began to have real feelings for one another, Akemi couldn't bring herself to leave Akai, even knowing his original motives.

Meanwhile, Akai infiltrated the syndicate under the code name of "Rye." Due to a slip-up by Andre Camel, his fellow agent, the syndicate discovered his true identity. From there, it was only a matter of time before the Black Organization also found out about Akai's relationship with Akemi, and took steps to eliminate both of them. Akemi was promised freedom for her sister in return for participating in an impossible bank heist, to make it easier to eliminate her when she inevitably failed.

Akai, on the other hand, was able to escape the syndicate's clutches, but is still haunted by his inability to save the love of his life — especially since it was due to his involvement that the syndicate ordered Akemi dead. It is his anger that drives his war against the Black Organization: anger at the syndicate, and anger at himself.

See glossary

One Billion Yen Robbery Case
Akai's past

See questions
20 21

T he FBI manages to captures a member of the evil organization. This priceless opportunity comes about as a result of an unrelated incident that begins as a petty nuisance.

Rena Mizunashi, a popular newscaster for Hiuri Television, comes to Kogoro Mori and asks him to catch the boy or girl who keeps pulling ring-and-run pranks at her house. Conan easily identifies the suspect, and learns something even more valuable in the process. Through a bug he plants in Rena Mizunashi's shoe, he picks up the strains of "Nanatsu no Ko," proving that Mizunashi is a member of the Black Organization.

On that day, the syndicate plans an important operation. Koki Domon, a politician taking a hard stance against crime, is seen as a hindrance to the syndicate's plans. Rena Mizunashi, known within the syndicate as Kir, schedules an outdoor interview to put Domon in a position where snipers Chianti and Korn can get a clear shot.

Conan learns of the plan through the bug in Kir's shoe and alerts Agent Starling, who succeeds in foiling the assassination attempt. In the ensuing high-speed chase between the FBI and the Black Organization assassins, Kir crashes her motorcycle and sinks into a coma.

FBI agents are holding the comatose Kir at a selected hospital while they wait for her to regain consciousness, leading to a struggle between the FBI and the Black Organization for possession of the comatose woman.

⑤ee glossary

Black Impact! The Black Organization Is Within Reach! Hidemi Hondou

See questions
30 40 41 42

40 *What is Rena Mizunashi's true identity?*

The FBI isn't the only agency with a member inside the Black Organization. The CIA has placed Hidemi Hondou, a female Japanese spy, within the syndicate. Her public identity is newscaster Rena Mizunashi, and her codename within the organization is Kir.

Originally, Hidemi was working alongside her father Ethan, a Japanese-American who had also infiltrated the syndicate. However, syndicate operatives came very close to learning the pair's identity, and Ethan made a desperate attempt to save his daughter's life. He committed suicide, staging the scene so that it would look like Hidemi had killed him in the service of the Black Organization. In this way, he was able to save his daughter's life while ensuring that she could continue her undercover work for the CIA.

The plan was a success, and Hidemi

became highly regarded within the syndicate as a spy hunter. As she completed more missions for the Black Organization, she was rewarded with the codename of "Kir."

Currently, her status within the syndicate is still in jeopardy, particularly since Vermouth knows her true identity as a CIA agent. For now, however, Vermouth's peculiar loyalties and penchant for keeping secrets are keeping Kir alive.

See glossary

Ethan Hondou

See questions
34 41 42

Who is the student that transferred into Ran's class?

Eisuke Hondou, a new arrival to Ran and Sonoko's class at Teitan High School, is a male transfer student who supposedly resembles the newscaster Rena Mizunashi. The clumsy boy is always tripping over things, bumping into people, and getting into unfortunate accidents. During camping trips, he is always the first to be bitten by mosquitoes, and in group photos he is invariably the only one to have his eyes closed. Some students even believe that if he drops a piece of toast, it is guaranteed to land butter-side-down.

He is a fan of Kogoro Mori and begs to be taken to the scene of Mori's investigations. There, the clumsy boy shows a more observant side as he immediately notices Conan's vital role in the investigation, which startles and unsettles Conan.

After that awkward incident, Eisuke continues flattering Kogoro to win his trust and an apprentice position at the Mori

See glossary

The Irreversible Two

See questions
42

Detective Agency. Conan, however, is still reluctant to trust the strange boy...

What is Eisuke Hondou plotting?

> **Warning:** This section contains spoilers. If you'd rather wait to learn information vital to the story of Case Closed, skip to the next page/section.

Eisuke Hondou asked Ran if he could be her father's apprentice with clear goals in mind. To find his missing sister, he needed to be around Kogoro and his information sources and learn everything he could. As should be clear by now, his sister is the CIA spy Hidemi Hondou.

Even though a popular newscaster by the name of Rena Mizunashi looks exactly like his sister, he refuses to believe it could be her for quite some time. For a while, he even thought that this woman had murdered his sister, and then altered her own face to take her place. This wild theory comes largely from him knowing that the newscaster's blood type is AB, but he's convinced his sister is blood type O. When he was a child, his sister gave blood for him when he needed a transfusion, and he is type O, and therefore could only use the same type blood. This supposition falls apart

See glossary

The Irreversible Two
The Sealed Ocean Window
The Shadow of the Black Organization: The Mystery of the Big Reward and the Shining Star of Pearl
The Whereabouts of the Dark Photograph
The Truth Behind the Mistaken Phone Call
Murder Case from the Nether World

See questions
41

when it is revealed that his own blood type had changed after a bone marrow transplant, and he is in fact type AB.

While the FBI and the Black Organization fight over who controls his sister, Eisuke is finally able to reunite with her.

Chapter 03

Conan's adventures continue

Who is the Phantom Thief Kid?

P hantom Thief Kid is Conan's greatest adversary, though not in the sense that the Black Organization is. Always seen in a snow white cape, silk hat, and monocle, the age and real name of this master thief are completely unknown. His rivalry with Conan is equivalent to Lupin vs. Holmes.

Commonly known as "Kid," he is known by police as "Phantom Thief No. 1412." This name originates from a misreading of the number 1412 by Shinichi's father, written in such haste that it more resembled the word KID.

He specializes in stealing art works and jewels, but always declares his target publicly before performing the actual heists. Because of a strong chivalrous streak, stealing mere money goes against his sense of propriety.

In fact, the Phantom Thief Kid stars in his own manga series called Magic Kaito, also by Gosho Aoyama. Kaito Kuroba and

the Phantom Thief Kid are one and the same person. He first appeared in Case Closed as a one-time cameo, but fans liked him so much, he's now a regular in the series.

It's a family tradition to perform magic, and this is likely why he finds such pleasure in fooling the police time and time again. As a master of disguise, he can make himself appear to be a man or woman of any age, and once even pretended to be Ran so convincingly that Conan never suspected the truth.

While many characters in Case Closed have a flair for the dramatic that goes far into the realms of corny, the Phantom Thief Kid is especially prolific. During his first encounter with Conan, he declares "Don't you know? The Phantom Thief is an artist, stealing in the most creative fashion, leaving the detective as a mere critic, struggling to find flaws." Conan responds in kind, saying "I'll pay my respects to that artist who slipped through security by facing him one on one. All artists are famous the day after they die, and I'll make you famous, Phantom Thief Kid. Your grave will be prison."

See glossary

Conan vs. the Phantom Thief Kid
Magic Lover's Murder Case
The Gathered Detectives!
Shinichi Kudo vs. Phantom Thief Kid
Phantom Thief Kid's Miraculous Aerial Walk
Big Adventure in the Eccentric Mansion
Phantom Thief Kid and the Four Masterpieces

See questions
15 16

44 | *Then what about the first Phantom Thief Kid?*

To most, there is only one Phantom Thief Kid, but Kaito Kuroba is in fact the second to use the name. Phantom Thief Kid's first appearance was in Paris, 18 years previous, and marked the beginning of a long series of heists. Then, 8 years before the current story arc, he disappeared. This was the work of Touichi Kuroba, Kaito's father.

Rivalry between the Kudo and Kuroba families is nothing new. Battles between Yusaku and Touichi in their prime were even more intense than the encounters between their sons today, ever divided between thief and protector.

Years ago, when Shinichi was in 1st grade, Kid left a written challenge encrypted in a cipher. He expected Shinichi would give up and take it to his father for help, but young Shinichi was more determined and persistent than even Kid could imagine. Even though Shinichi's peers still had trouble reading common kanji characters, he came within one

See glossary

Shinichi Kudo's Childhood Adventure

See questions
15 16 43

100

step of finding the solution to the cipher. To this day, Shinichi loves cryptograms, perhaps because of this early experience with Kid.

45 Is there anything Conan can't do?

Particularly when Shinichi is his normal self, it seems like he can do it all. Until it comes to music, that is. Whether he's Conan or Shinichi, his singing is so horrible it turns the stomach of anyone in earshot. Even when dealing with codes, normally one of his fortes, if it involves musical notation or knowledge of music, he has great trouble grasping the solution. This is usually when Ran steps in to assist, using her piano skills to help him out.

He can identify songs fairly reliably, but he's oblivious to trends in popular music. And while not completely tone deaf, he seems incapable of creating the correct notes in any form. So where did he inherit this from, his mother or his father?

See glossary

Karaoke Parlor Murder Case

See questions

2

PTX 4869 is an experimental drug developed by the Black Organization, and intended for assassinations. Because it disappears quickly from the body of the victim after death, it gives the impression that the victim died of natural causes. It works by destroying the body's cells.

Prof. Miyano conducted research and testing for the drug from the beginning of the project, and after his death, his daughter Shiho (Ai Haibara) continues his work.

The drug had only been tested on animals, but Shiho withheld the fact that in some cases it did not kill but instead shrank the victim to an earlier stage of life. By the time testing was conducted, her loyalty to the Black Organization had begun to waver, so she said nothing about this abnormal result.

After the drug had been forced on Shinichi Kudo, his home was searched for any sign he'd survived. It was discovered that most

of his children's clothes had gone missing, but since Shiho was the only person to know about the shrinking effect, nothing more was thought of this fact.

Still, Shiho only thought this was a rare side-effect, and not that the chance of recurrence is high. So when Shiho tried to kill herself, she ingested what she thought was a lethal dose of APTX 4869. Instead, she found herself shrunk as well.

Is this really a chance side-effect? Or do Shinichi and Shiho share a rare trait that triggers it?

See glossary
APTX4869
Baijiu

See questions				
1	4	20	21	27
33	37			

47 Why does murder follow Conan wherever he goes?

Perhaps it is the destiny of a detective, or something more complex. Either way, murder and mystery always find Conan, whether he goes to the beach, camping, or simply to a school festival. The grim reaper himself seems to have his eye on Conan Edogawa.

Early in the series, Conan is happy to demonstrate his skill and reasoning at every opportunity. It doesn't take long for it to turn into a routine, and he begins to regard these cases as a part of a normal life. Kogoro Mori still thinks it odd, and he sees most of the cases just because he's usually around Conan.

This habit of being the first to report a murder has earned Kogoro the nickname of "angel of death," at least according to Inspector Megure. But given that incidents always find Conan, even when Kogoro isn't around, it seems Conan is the determining factor.

But which is it really? Does Conan attract trouble, or does trouble attract Conan?

See glossary

Juzo Megure

See questions
4 17 26 27

Traditionally in Japanese detective stories, the guilty party dies, whether by their own hand or karmic circumstances. One such example is the Kindaichi Case Files, created by Seishi Yokomizo.

The main character, Kosuke Kindaichi, always solves the mystery, and the criminal usually commits suicide after being revealed. It was still a popular series, but fans came to expect this format. Most characters in the stories were of a more traditional or archaic frame of mind, and saw this as the only recourse after their crimes. Occasionally Kindaichi makes an attempt to stop these events, but in the end relents, reasoning that perhaps it's better to die than live a life of shame. So every solved case usually produced yet another death.

This pattern is common even in modern mystery stories, and is almost considered classic for a culprit to throw himself or herself

off a cliff in Japanese detective dramas and comics.

In contrast to this tradition, Conan Edogawa believes that solving the crime is not a detective's only concern. Rather, a detective should seek to protect every life he can, regardless of what has been done by whom. Every life is equal and worth saving. To him, allowing a culprit to die is tantamount to murder.

This is probably why Heiji Hattori and Conan get along so well, for they both hold to these tenets. Even when Heiji was criticized for saving a victim and damaging a crime scene, Conan respected him for it.

Try as he might, even Conan can't follow his own beliefs every time. Only once did a culprit in one of his cases die. The suspect set fire to a house and ended up burning to death inside, and Conan could do nothing to stop it. This incident haunts him, particularly when anyone attempts suicide.

⑤ee glossary

Moonlight Sonata Murder Case

What is the author of Case Closed like?

Born on June 21, 1963, Gosho Aoyama is from Tottori Prefecture and the second eldest of four brothers. His older brother became a scientist, his younger brother runs the family repair business, and his youngest brother is now a physician. Their technical and scientific specialties are a wonderful resource to Aoyama when he crafts tricks and stories for *Case Closed*.

As a child, Aoyama loved trivia and solving puzzles, and could even figure out directions in the woods from a tree stump, much like a member of the Junior Detective League. He describes himself as a child as "Conan in a good way, and Mitsuhiko in a bad way."

Some of the tricks in his stories come from his childhood games. Classic works like Sherlock Holmes and Lupin (Arsène Lupin, not Lupin III) were important influences on him in his early years.

These influences helped shape his imagination and stories. His parents hated comics, so he focused his efforts on becoming an art teacher and studied at Nihon University. While there, he joined the Comic Researchers Club. An older classmate was trying to make it as a professional comic author, and Aoyama did what he could to help. This led to Aoyama's first published work, and he debuted as an author in 1986 highly regarded by his publisher.

Magic Kaito was his first big hit (and first appearance of the Phantom Thief Kid), as well as *YAIBA!*, a period drama comic. His third major work is the series *Case Closed*, the first installment of which was published after only two weeks of conception and development. The starting point for *Case Closed* was the creation of the character design for Conan in his trademark glasses and bow tie.

See glossary

The Gathered Detectives!
Shinichi Kudo vs. Phantom
Thief Kid

See questions
50

50 Where does Aoyama get his tricks?

Mystery fans regard the tricks in *Case Closed* very highly because no matter how absurd they may seem at first glance, nearly all of them are based on real possibilities. Aoyama has even said that he finds hints for his tricks in daily life. Additionally, tricks are refined by both Aoyama and his editor.

In a fan book interview, he said: "I've said to people, 'you're holding the receiver with your left hand, aren't you?' over the phone and they're very surprised that I was right. I revealed to them, 'That's because you pressed the buttons with your right.' It's important to notice these small things in your daily lives that most people would overlook. Whenever you come across a situation that would make you go 'you got me!' it would make it all the more interesting. That's why I'm always on the lookout for those things."

Sometime the tricks take a lot of research to portray them accurately, and he even does

on site research. Once, he needed to visit the actual Metropolitan Police Department, but feared a cold reception because the police force is so often seen as dependent on the detectives in the series. To his surprise, police officers there gave him a warm welcome and even asked for his autograph. Just more proof that all kinds of people love *Case Closed*.

See glossary

Misao Yamamura

See questions
49

51 How many cases has Conan solved so far?

As of November 2007, *Case Closed* has 59 manga volumes available in Japan and a total of 178 cases. Not all are solved by Conan, but even considering that, it's quite an impressive number.

Based on conversations between Heiji and Conan, readers are led to believe that Conan handles more cases than the ones that make it into the series. This makes it impossible to put an exact number on mysteries Conan has solved, but whatever that number is, it's a credit to his abilities as a detective.

Crimes scenes run the range from Western aristocratic mansions, Japanese-style rooms with *shoji* and *fusuma* sliding doors, sports stadiums, and even theaters and theme parks. Each scene is populated by a unique community of people, both friend and foe alike.

This variety is something Aoyama loves about the mystery genre. He told *Sankei Shimbun* in October 2007, "Mystery works

are interesting because you can include many different genres. For example, many different worlds can be used; like if the culprit is an athlete, you can use the sports world, and if the culprit is an actor, you can use the world of show business. Personally, I find it refreshing to be able to use many different settings so that it will never become boring."

Aoyama's love of these myriad settings and his penchant for cryptograms and codes can be seen throughout the series. He's also named the episode that brings Officers Takagi and Sato together during a bomb threat a favorite episode in the series.

See glossary

The Trembling MPD: Twelve Million Hostages

See questions
25

Conan Edogawa has a particularly extensive library of catchphrases and sayings that he enjoys using most. This canon of lines is popular among school children imitating Conan; some of the most famous are listed below.

"I'm Conan Edogawa, the detective!"

Perhaps his most well-known catchphrase, it is his typical response to the cornered wrongdoer faced with the child detective. He avoids using it in front of Ran or Kogoro for fear of being found out.

"There is always only one truth!"

A common thing to hear in the anime series and movies, and is usually found at the end of an episode preview.

"Baaro" (Idiot)

Short for "Baka yarou" (idiot), Conan uses this version whenever he can. Normally, the

only ones to shorten it this way are middle-aged men who've had too much to drink, but with the popularity of *Case Closed*, children all over Japan have taken up this phrase.

"Hey, what's that?"

Conan uses this phrase to call attention to important evidence so adults at a crime scene won't miss an important clue. Other members of the Junior Detective League hate to hear him speak so childishly because it is so unlike his normal manner. Mitsuhiko once confronted him about it, demanding to know why he acts like that in front of adults.

Bonus Mottos:

"When you have eliminated the impossible, whatever remains, however improbable, must be the truth."

This is said by Sherlock Holmes in "The Sign of the Four." Shinichi also uses the same motto as a detective because he respects Holmes more than anybody else.

(Conan and Shinichi's famous lines)

"Tricks are nothing but puzzles devised by humans. If humans used their heads, they can logically find the answer... But unfortunately, no matter how I rack my brain, I can't figure out why humans would kill other humans ... Even if I understand why, I don't want to accept it..."

"You don't need a reason. I don't know about why people would want to kill other people, but there isn't a logical reason why people would want to help other people!"

See glossary

And There Were No Mermaids
Shinichi Kudo N.Y. (New York) Case

See questions
3 **5**

Which Case Closed movie is the best?

*C*ase Closed has 12 movies, the first of which, "The Time-Bombed Skyscraper," came out in 1998. Each movie tends to come out in late April, just in time for a holiday break in Japan that lasts from April to early May.

Among the 12 movies, the most popular to date has been "Detective Conan: The Phantom of Baker Street." The script for the original story was written by Hisashi Nozawa, famous for writing "Violent Cop," Kitano Takeshi Kitano's first movie.

The plot revolves around a virtual reality game based on a story written by Yusaku Kudo, set in 19th century London, including appearance by Sherlock Holmes and Jack the Ripper. Murders in the real world begin happening in sync with deaths in the game, leading Conan and all the regular characters to get drawn into a mystery so dangerous that even they aren't safe from death. While popular, the tone of the movie is different

enough from the series that many fans consider it an unconventional representation of *Case Closed*.

Unrepresentative or not, the movie placed second in overall box office rankings for 2002.

See glossary

Yusaku Kudo

See questions				
8	9	10	24	24

Heizo Hattori is the chief commissioner and Superintendent Supervisor of the Osaka Police Department, one of the highest positions a police officer can attain. Naturally, he passed the Public Servant Type 1 Exam and is considered a career police officer.

Usually stoic and a bit sour in expression, he's famous for running a very tight shift and is known in the Kansai region by criminals as "Heizo the Ogre" as a result of his ruthless crackdowns. He isn't seen very often in the series, but is said to have deductive abilities on par with Yusaku Kudo.

Ranked among the strongest kendo masters in Japan, he has made sure his son follows in his footsteps and studies the martial art. Even at home, he seems cold and distant, but plays the stern father because he believes that it is best for his son to become a real man.

He understands his son a bit too well, and used Heiji's propensity to lose his temper in

order to flush out criminals at Osaka Castle. The plan was a success, but his wife is furious with him for it.

Heizo's best friend Toyama is a childhood friend now working as his subordinate in the police department. Toyama is Kazuha's father, who grew up with Heiji. Toyama would be pleased to see his daughter marry his best friend's son instead of some stranger. Heiji and Kazuha are unaware, but Toyama and Heizo have discussed at length the possibility of them as a match.

See glossary

Osaka Double Mystery: The Swordsman and Taiko Castle (2)

See questions
22 23

Inspector Megure feels that needing Conan and Kogoro's help to solve cases marks him as an inferior detective, but he really isn't incompetent at all. What he doesn't quite realize is that his true talent is his leadership, utilizing his team as if they were extensions of his own self. His title in Section 1 is more suited to him than he realizes.

Very few people have ever seen him not wearing his brown trench coat and hat. He wears these things always in an attempt to hide his middle-age spread, but how does sleeping in his hat accomplish this?

The Junior Detective League comes up with new theories all the time, from hiding thinning hair to covering a bump on his head. The true reason is much more complicated. Over 20 years ago, when Megure was a rookie, high school girls were being targeted by a hit-and-run killer. The police ran out of leads, but one student volunteered to be a

decoy after her friend was murdered by the killer. Though the police at first refused, they finally allowed her to play decoy with Megure as her protection. Sure enough, the killer tried to run over both Megure and the girl.

According to his superior, Superintendent Matsumoto, "Megure only suffered injuries to his eye, but the student was nearly dead by the time the others got to them." Fortunately, the culprit was finally arrested, but Megure still has a scar on his head from that incident. He continues to wear his hat for fear of anyone asking about the scar.

This is not for guilt over a young girl's death, because the girl survived. She is now Inspector Megure's wife, Midori. Embarrassed by this story, he hides the scar, knowing if he explains its origin, it will inevitably lead to how he and Midori first met.

Despite it all, he is intensely devoted to his wife, even if he believes his reputation as a tough cop would be ruined if anyone sees her with him.

See questions
24

C onan's trademark glasses are only for show and an effort to prevent anyone from recognizing him for who he truly is. Thanks to Prof. Agasa, they are not merely cosmetic, for he has incorporated unique inventions into the glasses.

Whenever a bug is planted on someone, the glasses (when a button on the left earpiece is pressed, an antenna will pop up) can track the target. It is especially useful against the Black Organization. The only problem it has is that its battery life is far too short. An infrared telescope was added on later to make it even more high tech.

Furthermore, the transmitter that comes with the glasses looks like a sticker, and can be stuck on anything and anyone. Conan usually keeps it on the button of his jacket. It has a range of up to 20 km.

S ee glossary

Suspect Pursuit Glasses

See questions
5 11

57 | *What happens if the Tranquilizer Watch misses the target?*

The Tranquilizer Watch only has one shot, so if Conan misses his intended target, he must find a different method to solve the case. He usually uses it to explain a mystery, so he rarely uses it on a suspect, especially since a moving target is much harder to hit. If he does miss and can't use someone to reveal the solution, he's been known to feed Kogoro enough clues to lead him to the answer. Because this takes so much longer, he's very careful not to miss.

Some worry about these spent darts lying around and becoming a hazard to others or the environment, but Aoyama has stated that the material the darts are made of is environmentally friendly and therefore doesn't require Conan to constantly search for spent darts.

ee glossary

Watch Tranquilizer Gun
Kogoro Mori
Sonoko Suzuki

See questions
11

Which real-life celebrities have appeared in Case Closed?

The most famous real-life celebrity to appear in Case Closed is TV personality Takashi Matsuo, who made a guest appearance as the baddie. Matsuo actually asked Aoyama to make him the "bad guy."

For the episode, Matsuo played a television personality about to get fired by the producer because of low ratings. Matsuo kills the producer during the filming of a show and tries to create the perfect alibi as Conan and Kogoro look on. The producer Michihiko Suwa played himself in the episode.

You also may not be aware that the voice actress for Conan, Minami Takayama, is part of TWO-MIX, a well-known music duo in Japan. In one scene, she sings one of her own songs, but has to sing it badly since Conan can't sing.

Many other characters have been inspired by other famous people, but the only direct appearances are the three mentioned above.

See glossary

TV Station Murder Case
The Devil at the TV Station
The Kidnapping of a Popular
Musician

Since the series is still going strong, the possibility of celebrity cameos is always there.

I n the beginning, only Prof. Agasa knows that Conan is really Shinichi Kudo. Inevitably, Shinichi's parents are next to learn the truth, shortly followed by Heiji, after Conan fails to put Heiji to sleep and use him to solve a case.

Ai Haibara knows Conan's secret partly because she helped create the drug that shrank him and subsequently suffered its effects as well. While the Black Organization doesn't know of the side effects or Haibara's or Conan's identities, one of their members, Vermouth, discovers the truth after spying on Conan and Ran.

The FBI is protecting Conan and Haibara from Vermouth, but Conan still hasn't told Jodie and Shuichi Akai, the center of the team, about his secret.

The seventh and final person to know about Conan is Eisuke Hondou, who deduces the truth simply through observation and reasoning.

Officially, only these seven know Conan

Edogawa is Shinichi Kudo (in the movie version, Phantom Thief Kid also learns the secret).

Who will find out next, and what consequences will it bring? Conan wants to tell Ran Mori more than anyone else in the world, but she's the last person he'll allow himself to tell, out of fear for her safety. When will he finally be able to tell her everything?

See glossary

Hiroshi Agasa
Yusaku Kudo
Yukiko Kudo
Heiji Hattori
Ai Haibara
Vermouth
Eisuke Hondou

See questions
14

GLOSSARY

Characters

Conan and the Kudo Family

Conan Edogawa

The main character of the series. The Black Organization forced him to ingest the potion APTX4869, which shrank his body to the size of a child's. He lives the life of an ordinary 6 year old—except that he also solves crimes with his ingenious deductive abilities.

Shinichi Kudo

Conan Edogawa's true form and previous identity, a famous 17-year-old high school student and detective. Now he appears mainly in flashback scenes and in rare cases when the effects of APTX4869 are suppressed.

Yusaku Kudo

Shinichi's father and a world-famous mystery novelist. His most famous work is the Night Baron series. He once assisted a detective in solving a difficult case and has the best deductive abilities of anyone in Case Closed.

Yukiko Kudo

Shinichi's mother. 37 years old. Her maiden name is Fujimine, and she was once a famous actress. She retired from show business when she married Yusaku. While an actress, she learned the art of disguise and became a master of it.

Mori Family

Ran Mori

The series' female lead and Shinichi's childhood friend. Though they love each other, neither of them has confessed it. She is a martial arts master, but

is afraid of ghosts.

Kogoro Mori

Ran Mori's father. 38 years old. He was once a police officer of Section One of the Metropolitan Police Department, but now he works as a private detective—an extremely inept one. Fortunately, Conan solves all his cases for him, making him famous in the process.

Eri Kisaki

Ran Mori's mother and Kogoro's wife. 37 years old and a skilled lawyer. She and Kogoro are currently separated, and at work she goes by her maiden name. They want to get back together, but they're both too stubborn and proud.

Hattori Family and others

Heiji Hattori

A 17-year-old Osaka resident, also known as the Great Detective of the West. He considers Shinichi his rival at first, but now they acknowledge one another's abilities and have become friends. He has a straightforward manner and loses his temper easily. He is a kendo master.

Heizo Hattori

Heiji's father and chief commissioner of the Osaka Police Department. He is feared as the "demon" of Kansai Prefecture because of his strict manner.

Shizuka Hattori

Heiji's mother and Heizo's wife. She is a beautiful woman who looks good in a kimono.

Kazuha Toyama

Heiji's childhood friend and girlfriend. She loves Heiji with all her heart, but their relationship has not progressed very far due to his obliviousness. She is an aikido master.

Toyama

Kazuha's father, whose given name is unknown. He is an old friend of Heizo's and is assistant commissioner of the Osaka Police.

Miyano Family

Ai Haibara

Her real name is Shiho Miyano. Under the code name "Sherry," she was formerly a researcher for the Black Organization. She fled after the organization murdered her sister. Although her real age is 18, she looks 6 because she took APTX4869, which she herself developed and created.

Akemi Miyano

Shiho's older sister. She grew up in the Black Organization but fell in love with undercover FBI agent Shuichi Akai. The Black Organization killed her to prevent a betrayal.

Atsushi Miyano

Akemi and Shiho's father. He was a researcher for the Black Organization and supposedly died in an accident years ago. He was good friends with Professor Agasa, but he always kept his research secret.

Elena Miyano

Shiho and Akemi's mother and Atsushi's wife. She is British. She supposedly died in the same accident that killed her husband.

Professor Agasa and the Junior Detective League

Hiroshi Agasa

A 52-year-old inventor and Shinichi's neighbor. He was the first person to whom Conan confessed his true identity. He has invented innumerable gadgets to aid Conan in his work.

Genta Kojima

Conan's classmate at Teitan Elementary School. Overweight and bossy, he is nonetheless the self-declared leader of the Junior Detective League. While none too bright, he is very observant.

Ayumi Yoshida

Conan's classmate and fellow member of the Junior Detective League. She has a mild and kind personality that makes her beloved by everyone. She loves animals and has a wild imagination.

Mitsuhiko Tsuburaya

Conan's classmate and yet another member of the Junior Detective League. He is an honor student with a wide knowledge of trivia. He was timid at first, but his participation in the Junior Detective League has given him strength and maturity.

Ran Mori's friends

Sonoko Suzuki

Ran's classmate at Teitan High School and Shinichi's acquaintance. The daughter of the head of the Suzuki Conglomerate. Though born into a rich family, her personality is unpretentious and frank. Conan often puts her to sleep, and has her be his voice as detective.

Makoto Kyogoku

Sonoko's boyfriend and captain of Teitan High School's karate team. He is one of the strongest martial artists in Japan. While strong enough to take on dozens of gangsters, he never understands jokes and is often clueless and absent-minded.

Eisuke Hondou

Ran's classmate. He is a self-proclaimed Kogoro fan, so he spends a lot of time at the detective agency. While clumsy, he has a keen sense of observation. He seems to be

searching for something.

Jodie Saintemillion

A 28-year-old American woman who took over the post of English teacher at Teitan High School, where she has become good friends with Ran and Sonoko. She said she came to Japan because of her love of games, but the truth is...

Yukiko Kudo's friends

Sharon Vineyard

An Oscar-winning American actress. She and Yukiko Kudo both studied under the magician Kuroba and became friends.

Chris Vineyard

Sharon Vineyard's daughter, who takes after her now-retired mother. Regarded as one of the best actresses in Hollywood.

Metropolitan Police Department Section 1

Juzo Megure

An MPD Section 1 inspector. He was once Kogoro Mori's superior but now commands the likes of Takagi and Sato at crime scenes. He always wears a hat.

Wataru Takagi

A young cop of MPD Section 1. He makes many mistakes and appears unreliable, but there is no one more trustworthy. He falls in love with Officer Sato, and they eventually start dating.

Miwako Sato

A lieutenant of MPD Section 1. Her open-hearted nature, coupled with her good looks, makes her popular all over the MPD. She overcame a traumatizing experience from three years ago and is now with Takagi.

Ninzaburo Shiratori

An inspector of MPD Section 1 and a member of the "career crew." He falls in love with Sato and tries to intervene between her and Takagi.

Jinpei Matsuda

A member of the bomb squad with Section 1 for only seven days before dying on duty in an accident. He was in a relationship with Sato.

Local Police

Sango Yokomizo

An inspector with the Shizuoka Prefectural Police transferred from the Saitama Prefectural Police. He has a gentle personality and respects Kogoro as a detective. His distinctive hairstyle resembles coral.

Jugo Yokomizo

Sango's twin brother and also an inspector, but of the Kanagawa Prefectural Police. Although identical to his elder brother, their personalities are exact opposites. He teases Kogoro by calling him "The Baffling Kogoro."

Misao Yamamura

An officer of the Gunma Prefectural Police and so incompetent that readers may wonder how he became a police officer. He deeply respects Kogoro and joined the police force because he was influenced by a police drama in which Shinichi's mother, Yukiko, once starred.

FBI

Jodie Starling

A 28-year-old female FBI agent and an expert marksman. Her mother was killed by Vermouth, an executive of the Black Organization, on whom Jodie then swore revenge.

Shuichi Akai

A first-rate sniper who can accurately pin a target from 700 yards away. He infiltrated the Black Organization while undercover, but a mistake got his lover, Akemi, killed.

James Black

FBI agent. Jodie and Akai's superior. He holds Conan's deductive abilities in high regard.

CIA

Hidemi Hondou

Eisuke Hondou's older sister and a CIA agent. She went undercover with the Black Organization and was given the code name "Kir." She also goes by the identity Rena Mizunashi, a reporter for Hiuri Television.

Ethan Hondou

CIA agent and father to Hidemi and Eisuke. He infiltrated the Black Organization with Hidemi, but

failed, and camouflaged his death in such a way that Hidemi was able to continue undercover.

Black Organization

That Person

The leader of the Black Organization, about whom nothing is known.

Gin

A central figure in the Black Organization. Extremely smart and sadistic, he thinks nothing of murdering others. He forced Shinichi Kudo to take APTX4869, which shrank Kudo to the size of a child.

Vodka

Gin's underling. He remembers the people that Gin kills and performs other supporting functions.

Vermouth

A female executive of the Black Organization and a favorite of That Person. She has a romantic relationship with Gin. She is hated by the rest of the organization because of her secretive ways. She appears to have her own plans for the syndicate.

Pisco

His true name is Kenzo Masuyama. To the public, he is the owner of a certain car company, but he has long been an executive of the Black Organization. He is a skilled sniper, but is executed on the orders of Gin for making a mistake on the job.

Calvados

A sniper for the Black Organization. He cooperates with Vermouth in an attempt to kill Sherry after she betrays the syndicate but is stopped by Shuichi Akai. He later commits suicide. It is said he harbored feelings for Vermouth.

Sherry

A former researcher of the Black Organization, Ai Haibara.

Suguru Itakura

A programmer hired by the Black Organization, which orders him to develop a certain program. He refuses on the grounds that it is a crime against humanity.

Others

Phantom Thief Kid

A jewel thief, well-known for always sending a note before committing a crime. He uses magician's tricks to evade the police and has had numerous epic battles with Conan. His true identity is Kaito Kuroba.

First Phantom Thief Kid

Kaito Kuroba's father, Touichi Kuroba, and a renowned magician in his time. He and Shinichi's father, Yusaku, were rivals.

APTX4869 (Apotoxin4869)

A powerful poison developed by the Black Organization. It destroys cells in the human body without leaving a trace. In rare cases, however, the body's cells simply shrink instead of being destroyed. This is what occurred in the cases of Conan and Ai Haibara.

Baijiu

A Chinese liquor made from grain. When those whose bodies have been shrunk by APTX4869 drink it to alleviate a fever, the effects of the poison are temporarily suppressed. Ai Haibara researches its properties and makes it into a temporary antidote to APTX4869.

Watch Tranquilizer Gun

A tranquilizer gun embedded in Conan's watch. A switch on the watch fires a dart that will knock out a target. Since it only contains one dart, Conan only has one try.

Bowtie Voice Changer

Conan uses this bowtie to imitate the voices of people he's knocked out, such as Kogoro or Sonoko. He uses this method to reveal his deductions and expose the culprit. As long as Conan has heard the person speak before, he can duplicate his or her voice.

Magnified Kicking Power Shoes

The sneakers Conan usually wears. They use electricity to stimulate certain acupressure points and allow Conan to kick much harder than he normally could.

Suspect Pursuit Glasses

Radar embedded in Conan's (purely cosmetic) glasses. The transmitter resembles a sticker, which Conan usually keeps on a button. Once the sticker has been transferred to a target, Conan can follow that person anywhere using his glasses.

DB Badge

A badge carried by the members of the Junior Detective League. (DB is short for Detective Boys.) Members can use it to communicate within a 12.5-mile radius.

Turbo Boosted Skateboard

A skateboard with a solar-powered booster engine. It is used to pursue suspects, but often breaks in the process.

Ball Discharging Belt

A belt that Conan usually wears. When triggered, the belt inflates and propels out a soccer ball made with a special type of reinforced rubber, which the skilled Conan can then use as a weapon. It can also be used to break a fall from high places.

Cases that appear in Case Closed

Roller Coaster Murder Case/The Big Shrink

The first case. Shinichi Kudo and Ran Mori are on a date at a theme park when they witness a decapitation. After solving the case, Shinichi follows two men in black, who turn out to be Gin and Vodka, and is forced to swallow APTX4869. This marks the first appearance of the Black Organization.

Company President's Daughter Kidnapping Case/Kidnapped Debutante

A small girl is kidnapped by a man clad in black—and Kogoro Mori is on the case! Conan tags along and discovers that the case began as a sham, but that the girl was later kidnapped by someone else for real. This is the first case Shuichi solves as Conan Edogawa.

An Idol's Locked Room Murder Case

Idol Yoko Okino, of whom Kogoro is an enormous fan, hires Kogoro and Conan to protect her from a stalker. Upon arrival, however, they discover the body of Yoko's old boyfriend in her room. Will they be able to prove her innocence?

The Man Who Was Followed

A man with a 500-million-yen life insurance policy has been murdered, and the suspect is the man who requested that Kogoro tail him. Conan examines the mystery via photographic evidence and picks apart the man's alibi. This is the first alibi breakdown to appear in Case Closed.

One-Billion-Yen Robbery Case

A young girl asks Kogoro to find her missing father—but the young girl turns out to be part of a ring of bank robbers who have stolen one billion yen! This case features the first appearance of Akemi Miyano, Ai Haibara's sister.

The Haunted House Case

After transferring to Teitan Elementary School, Conan goes with his classmates Genta, Ayumi and Mitsuhiko to a Western-style mansion that is reputed to be haunted. What started as a dare becomes a night of strange phenomena. The Junior Detective League forms for the very first time!

Luxury Liner Serial Murder Case

On the way back from a trip, Kogoro, Ran and Conan hitch a ride on a luxury cruise, where they meet the wealthy Hanamoto family. When bodies start turning up, they know only someone on the ship could have done it, but who?

Once-a-Month Present Threat Case/Case of the Mysterious Gifts

Ogawa, a surgeon, hires Kogoro for a very peculiar case: starting two years ago, someone has been sending him a used toy and one million yen in cash every month. And on August 3, he always receives morning glories! During the investigation, Ogawa's 5-year-old son is kidnapped.

Art Museum Owner Murder Case

Conan and Ran investigate rumors of a suit of armor that walks around by itself in the middle of the night at the Beikacho Art Museum. While they're there, the art museum owner is murdered and security footage shows the culprit wearing a full suit of armor!

Bullet Train Bomb Case/ The Time Bomb Express

Kogoro and company decide to take the bullet train, or Shinkansen, to a wedding in Kyoto. Conan spots the black-clad men who shrank his body there. While eavesdropping on their conversation, he discovers that they plan to blow up the entire train in order to assassinate one person on it!

The Coded Map of the City Case

The Junior Detective League visits Tokyo Tower, where someone takes Ayumi's bag by mistake. The bag left in its place contains a mysterious coded map.

Mountain Villa Mummy Murder Case

Conan and Ran are invited by Ran's friend, Sonoko Suzuki, to a reunion at the Suzuki summer home. Their fun is cut short when one of the friends is snatched by a mysterious bandaged man.

Karaoke Parlor Murder Case

Ran, Sonoko and Conan attend the final concert of pop band Rex, and witness the lead singer, Tatsuya Kimura, collapse after singing his last song. The cause of death: cyanide. A suicide note is found in his locker at the band's agency, but was it really suicide?

Conan Edogawa Kidnapping Case

A woman appears claiming to be Conan's mother, though Conan has never seen her before—and it isn't possible that "Conan Edogawa" could have a mother anyway! However, she knows his true identity. Could she be a part of the Black Organization?

The Antique Collector Murder Case

Kogoro, Ran and Conan go to a client's house to investigate a supposed extramarital affair only to find the client, a well-known antiques collector, dead. The crime

scene is scarred by deep cuts, as if the victim and the murderer had been fighting with swords!

Missing Corpse Murder Case

The Junior Detective League is asked to search for a missing cat, but the search turns up a human corpse! By the time they call the police, however, the body has already disappeared...

Tenkaichi Night Festival Murder Case

On the night of the Tenkaichi Night Festival, the novelist Sasai murders popular author Imatake, with whom he'd once been partners. In order to create an alibi, he'd had Conan, whom he'd met by chance earlier, take his picture. The picture clearly shows him with "Ten" and "ichi" appearing in the background. Since those words are lit only during certain times of the festival, the police are stumped. Conan, however, sees through to the truth of the matter. This is the first of many "inverted"

detective stories, in which the culprit is known from the beginning and the story progresses from the murderer's point of view.

Moonlight Sonata Murder Case

Kogoro and Conan receive a request from Keiji Asou, who lives on Getsuei Island. But when Conan, Ran and Kogoro arrive at the island, they discover that Keiji Asou died ten years ago! The mayoral elections begin, and various concerned parties start to die one by one...

Pro Soccer Player Blackmail Case

A female high school student shows up claiming to be Shinichi Kudo's ex-girlfriend and pleads for them to search for Shinichi. Ran is consumed by jealousy, but Conan has never seen this girl in his life. What is she up to?

Night Baron Murder Case

Conan, Ran and Kogoro take Professor Agasa's place in a mystery event held in Izu. Supposedly, they can win a very desirable prize if they can discover the whereabouts of the event's host. Then one of the participants falls out of the hotel and is impaled on a statue below. Just what have they gotten into?

A June Bride Murder Case

Ran, Sonoko and Shinichi's old middle school homeroom teacher, Sayuri Matsumoto, is getting married, but she's poisoned at her bridal shower! Who's trying to ruin the happiest day of Sayuri's life?

Ayumi Kidnapping Case

While playing hide-and-seek in the park with the other members of the Junior Detective League, Ayumi hides herself in the trunk of a car. The car drives off with Ayumi in the trunk, and the rest of the Junior Detective League tries to track her using their badges, only to find out that the car belongs to a kidnapper who specializes in abducting little girls!

Kogoro's Class Reunion Murder Case

Kogoro brings Ran and Conan to his university judo team reunion at a hot springs inn. When the former team manager, Yumi Horikoshi, is shot and killed, Kogoro burns with the need for justice. Understanding his feelings, Conan allows him to solve this one on his own.

Wealthy Daughter Murder Case

Reika, the daughter of the head of the Yotsui Group, invites Kogoro and company to her birthday party. When it's time to leave, however, they discover that their car has a flat, forcing them to stay the night with Reika and her potential suitors at the villa. During their stay, one of the potential grooms is murdered, and Ran is attacked.

Diplomat Murder Case

The Great Detective of the West, Heiji Hattori, comes all the way from Osaka to prove himself against Shinichi Kudo for the title of Great Detective of the East. Meanwhile, the wife of diplomat Isao Tsujimura asks the Mori Detective Agency to investigate her son's girlfriend. Heiji Hattori tags along. When they arrive at the Tsujimura household, they discover that Isao Tsujimura has been murdered! Heiji and Shinichi (who has temporarily returned to his true form thanks to the baijiu) compete to unravel the mystery.

Library Murder Case

The Junior Detective League heads to the library to help with Conan's book report but find a mystery instead: the head librarian has murdered one of the other librarians — and the body is somewhere in the library! Can the Junior Detective League find it?

Alpine Hut in the Snowy Mountain Murder Case

Conan, Ran and Kogoro meet Oyama, a university medical professor, while on a ski trip. After losing the key to their rented cottage, they stay with the generous Oyama. That night, Oyama is murdered—but he may have left a clue as to the identity of his murderer with his dying message!

TV Station Murder Case

Now that "The Sleeping Kogoro" is a famous detective, everyone knows his name and he even appears live on Takashi Matsuo's talk show. Matsuo takes advantage of the four minutes of pre-recorded footage to kill his producer, Suwa, and claims his live broadcast as his alibi. Too bad for him that Conan was in the audience! (Takashi Matsuo is a TV personality in real life.)

Coffee Shop Murder Case

Ran is in an extremely good

mood. Why? She says she's going on a date with Shinichi Kudo but Conan doesn't know anything about it! What's going on? He follows Ran on her date, only to discover a murder at the site. And who is the beautiful and intelligent woman he meets there? This episode features the first appearance of Eri Kisaki.

The Mist Goblin Legend Murder Case

While on the way back from cherry blossom viewing, Kogoro and company get another flat tire and spend the night at a Buddhist temple, where they hear a legend of flying mist goblins, or kiri-tengu. That night, one of the monks is killed and hung from a high ceiling. Could this be the work of the kiri-tengu?

The Secret of the Moon, the Star, and the Sun

The Junior Detective League and Professor Agasa head to Professor Agasa's uncle's summer home in search of a treasure he left behind. The treasure turns into a hunt Professor Agasa devised as a game for the children, but when they find the treasure they also find a mysterious cryptogram...

Game Company Murder Case

Conan attends a press conference at the Beika Hotel, where they are announcing a video game developed under the supervision of Kogoro Mori. There, he meets a man calling himself Tequila who mentions Gin and Vodka. Conan follows him, thinking he might have a connection to the Black Organization, but the man dies in an explosion. Could there be conflict within the Black Organization?

Holmes Freak Murder Case

Conan wins tickets to the Sherlock Holmes Freak Party, and a reluctant Kogoro attends with him. Heiji Hattori turns up as well. The host of the party is murdered, and Conan finds out the truth—

but Heiji finds out Conan's secret as well...

The Triplets' Country Home Murder Case

Ran and Conan visit Sonoko at her country home in Izu, where they meet her older sister, Ayako, and her fiancé, Yuzo Tomizawa. Tomizawa's father is present as well. But then Tomizawa's father is murdered by someone identical to Tomizawa. Tomizawa is the natural suspect, but then it turns out he's one of a set of triplets! Who is the real murderer?

An Illustrator Murder Case

The artist Kaneto Hanaoka murders his mistress and new assistant illustrator, Izumi Chono, before attending an interview with Kogoro Mori. He sets it up so that it appears that Izumi committed suicide during the interview. Conan quickly ascertains who the culprit is, but can he pick apart Kaneto's alibi?

Big Monster Gomera Murder Case

The Junior Detective League goes to see a filming of the newest installation of the popular monster movie series Gomera, and naturally, a murder occurs: the producer is killed by someone wearing the Gomera monster suit. Everyone there has a motive, because the producer has decided to cancel the Gomera series and the entire staff hates him.

Genius Magician Murder Case

When Conan falls asleep on the couch, Ran removes his glasses and notices that he bears a startling similarity to Shinichi. Later, a woman hires Kogoro to look into her husband's death. Her husband, a genius magician named Motoyasu Tsukomo, supposedly committed suicide, but she doesn't think this is the case. During the investigation, Ran comes close to finding out Conan's true identity...

Estate Heir Murder Case

Ran almost discovers Conan's true identity when she yells "Shinichi!" and Conan responds, but Conan and Shinichi's mother, Yukiko, are able to brush the incident off. The next day, Yukiko takes them to Gunma to visit an old friend. Meanwhile, a murder occurs at her home...

Ski Lodge Murder Case

Conan, Ran and Sonoko meet their former teacher, Akiko Yonehara, while on a ski trip. They're invited to her lodge, but get trapped there by a blizzard. Then Yonehara and Sonoko are assaulted by a serial killer!

The Kidnapping of a Popular Musician

The popular music duo TWO-MIX are staging a concert at Nippon Budokan, and the Junior Detective League ends up dining with singer Minami Takayama. But when her partner, Shiina Nagano, doesn't show, she goes out looking for him — and ends up getting kidnapped!

The Loan Company President's Murder Case

Kogoro takes Conan to meet his regular mahjong partner, the president of a loan company. When he doesn't show, they find him murdered in his locked office.

Honorable Family Serial Murder Case

Dosan Nagato, the head of the Nagato Group, hires Kogoro to find his first love. When they arrive at his home, they meet his first son, Hideomi, who suffers from hideous burns on his face. Later they find Dosan's daughter's husband and Hideomi both dead, along with a suicide letter, but Conan suspects murder...

The Seven Wonders of Teitan Elementary Case

The Staring Statue and the Vanishing Vice Principal are among

the Seven Wonders of Teitan Elementary. The Junior Detective League sets out to verify these wonders for itself.

Conan vs. the Phantom Thief Kid

The Phantom Thief Kid sends a coded message announcing that he will steal the Suzuki black pearl. Conan, after deciphering the code, awaits the Phantom Thief Kid atop the roof of the building. It's the first showdown between Conan and the Phantom Thief Kid!

The Famous Potter Murder Case

The potter Kikuemon, widely acknowledged to be a national treasure, invites Kogoro to his studio. While he's giving Kogoro a tour, his daughter-in-law accidentally breaks one of his masterpieces. The next day, her body is discovered in the studio. Did she kill herself out of guilt, or was it something else?

Scuba Diving Murder Case

Kogoro and his wife, Eri, have been separated for a while now. Ran made a bid to get them back together, but the two have been doing nothing but arguing. Through sheer coincidence, they end up dining with a group of college students who are fans of Kogoro. While scuba diving, one of them is bitten by a sea snake and dies. Was it an accident, or was it planned? Will Eri and Kogoro get back together?

Hospitalized Burglary Suspect Case

The Junior Detective League visits Kogoro at the hospital after he injures himself. Conan notices something strange about Sekiguchi, the man sharing Kogoro's room, and discovers that Sekiguchi's daughter has been kidnapped and will not be released until he kills someone in this hospital. Will the Junior Detective League be able to stop the crime and get the girl back?

The Mysterious Robbers and Mansion Case

Kogoro receives a mysterious note: the sender wants him to solve the mystery of a Western-style mansion that was left to him by his grandfather, a skilled watchmaker. What awaits Kogoro and Conan, however, is a mansion filled with bizarre tricks and devices...

Historical Play Performer Murder Case

Kogoro and company are invited to the actor Hijikata's house and receive some pointers on acting. Rumors have been swirling about Hijikata divorcing his wife, Isami. When Isami is murdered, her boyfriend, Okita, is suspected. Wataru Takagi of the Metropolitan Police Department makes his first appearance here.

The Memories of First Love Case

Ran and Sonoko are invited to Asami Uchida's party. After hearing that Asami was Shinichi's first love, Ran becomes jealous. But that all changes when Asami's house is set on fire...

The Girl from the Black Organization

Ai Haibara transfers to Teitan Elementary and is welcomed into the Junior Detective League. When they receive a request from a classmate to find his older brother, they discover that he was kidnapped by a woman in black. Feeling that the Black Organization is behind this, Conan tries to get the Junior Detective League to turn back, but...

University Professor Murder Case

It turns out Ai Haibara was once part of the Black Organization. She fled to Conan seeking help after her sister was murdered. They visit the house of a university professor who supposedly has information on APTX4869, but when they get there, he's been murdered...

Mystery Writer Disappearance Case

Nintaro Shinmei, a mystery writer, disappeared two months ago, and his daughter hires Kogoro to find him. Everyone is puzzled when they discover his manuscripts are still turning up at the publisher! Could there be a clue contained within them?

The Naniwa Serial Murder Case

Heiji Hattori invites Conan and company to Osaka. Bothered by a dream in which Shinichi was stabbed to death, he's made plans for them to tour in a patrol car. They don't get very far, though, when a body lands on the hood of the car! This episode features the first appearance of Toyama Kazuha.

Stadium Indiscriminate Threat Case

The Junior Detective League is enjoying a soccer game at the National Stadium when the ball is suddenly destroyed by a gunshot. The unseen sniper takes the stadium hostage for a 50-million-yen ransom, threatening to shoot indiscriminately if they stop the game or let the audience leave. Can Conan figure out where he is?

Magic Lover's Murder Case

Sonoko is a member of the Magic Lover's Club, and Ran joins her for a meeting at the clubhouse. Conan, not feeling well, leaves early with Kogoro, but they turn around in a hurry when they hear over the radio that someone at the clubhouse has been murdered. When they get there, they discover that the bridge to the clubhouse has been burned, leaving them isolated on the other side...

The Locked Bathroom Murder Case

Kogoro lost his ticket to a Yoko Okino concert! Fortunately, he meets a woman who says she'll give him her ticket as long as he picks up her sister. When he gets

to her house, however, he finds the sister dead in the bathroom!

The Old Blue Castle Investigation Case

The Junior Detective League and Professor Agasa go camping, but they forget to bring a tent! They find a mansion hidden deep in the woods and ask to stay the night. The owner's mother-in-law agrees, as long as they solve the mystery of the castle. During the investigation, each member disappears one by one, until only Ai and Ayumi are left...

The Flying Locked-Room! Shinichi Kudo's First Case

The Junior Detective League joins the professor on a plane trip, and Ran reminisces about a murder case that happened one year ago while she was on a trip with Shinichi. That was Shinichi's first case as a detective.

Metropolitan Police Detective Love Story

The Junior Detective League is called in as witness to the old castle incident. Meanwhile, a witness to a bank robbery is also summoned. When she doesn't show, Officer Takagi calls her at home and hears a scream through the phone. Miwako Sato, the idol of the MPD, makes her first appearance!

The Night Before the Wedding Locked-Room Case

Heiji attends a wedding in Tokyo and goes with Conan and the others to visit Meiji Shrine, where he meets the bride. She invites them to her home, where they stumble across a locked-room murder.

The North Star No. 3 Leaving Ueno

Conan and company go on a trip to Hokkaido on the overnight sleeper train, the North Star. While

on the train, a murder occurs that is identical to one of the plots of Shinichi's father's novels! Yusaku makes a long-desired reappearance here and shows off his superior detective skills.

Sonoko's Dangerous Summer Story

Sonoko goes to the beach with Ran, but for whatever reason the men are only interested in Ran! Finally a guy appears who seems to be interested in Sonoko, but the fun turns out to be short-lived because dead women suddenly start turning up. They've been cut up with knives. Karate expert Makoto Kyogoku makes his first appearance!

The Final Screening Murder Case

The Junior Detective League attends a screening of Gomera at a local theater that's going to be closed. During the screening, a corpse is discovered hanging in the theater! It's the real estate agent who purchased the theater's land!

The 20-Year Old Murder Case: The Symphony Serial Murders

Kogoro and company are on a trip to the Ogasawara Islands when they discover that Heiji Hattori and Kogoro's old boss, Samezaki, are also on the ship. Upon looking at the list of passengers, they discover that Kano, a robber who stole 400 million yen, is also on board. The statute of limitations is about to run out on his case, and Samezaki's looking for justice...

Metropolitan Police Detective Love Story 2

The Junior Detectives are practicing their acting in an abandoned building when Officer Sato suddenly charges in, pursuing a suspect. Sato is able to detain him, but the man insists that he's innocent. The Junior Detective League begins its own investigation with Officer Takagi...

The Blind Spot in the Darkness

Conan and Ran go to Araide Hospital to find out the results of a test Kogoro underwent. When they all come back negative, they decide to have a celebratory dinner. Dr. Araide's son, Tomoaki, seems to have fallen for Ran, and Conan is irritated and distressed. But then he has more than that to worry about when there's a blackout!

Reuniting with the Black Organization

Haibara has a dream in which she is killed by Gin, and the next day she sees Gin's car, a black Porsche. Conan places a transmitter on the car, and they tail it to a hotel where a powerful politician is assassinated. The episode features the first appearance of Pisco of the Black Organization.

The Revival of the Dying Message

While enjoying fireworks at the skating rink, one of their schoolmates is murdered by a shotgun blast! He left a mysterious message behind on his cell phone.

The Tottori Spider Mansion Demon

Kogoro and company are hired to investigate a murder that occurred three years ago at the Takeda household in Tottori, where they run into Heiji and Kazuha. The place has been dubbed the "Spider Mansion" by the locals, thanks to the large number of gruesome incidents that have happened there in the past. Well, they're about to be witness to one more...

The Desperate Revival: The Cavern of the Detective Boys

While camping in the mountains, the Junior Detective League discovers a limestone cave. In

search of treasure, they encounter some men hiding a body instead. While escaping, Conan is shot in the side and left in critical condition. Will the Junior Detective League be able to get him out in time?

Revival at the Risk of Death: The Wounded Great Detective

Convinced that Conan is Shinichi, Ran volunteers to give him her blood. Conan believes he may have no choice but to reveal his identity...

Revival at the Risk of Death, the Black Knight

Ran stars in a play at her school's Campus Festival. One of the alumni dies during the performance. The police rule it a suicide, and Shinichi— not Conan—makes an appearance to solve the case...

Revival at the Risk of Death, Shinichi's Return

Shinichi asks Ran out to a restaurant with the intent to propose, but a pesky murder case gets in the way. Knowing that time is running out, he nonetheless puts his deductive skills to the test...

The Significant Music Box

A college student asks Kogoro to find her missing pager friend. Conan deciphers the coded pager message and also discovers the location of the friend's house, where they find something unexpected...

Kogoro Mori, Suspect

Kogoro and company flee to Karuizawa to escape the summer heat, where they meet Eri and her coworkers. One of them is later found dead in her hotel room— along with Kogoro, who's drunk! Can Conan and the others keep Kogoro from facing jail time?

Metropolitan Police Detective Love Story 3

Today is the anniversary of Officer Sato's father's death. He was chasing a robber when he was hit by a truck and killed. The statute of limitations on the crime has already run out, but Officer Takagi discovers the truth. But before he can tell Officer Sato...

The Battle Game Trap

Ran and the others are at the arcade after school when their new English teacher, Jodie Saintemillion, appears. While she watches two people playing a fighting game, one of them suddenly dies!

Mushrooms, Bears, and the Junior Detective League

While out foraging for matsutake mushrooms, Genta wanders away from the rest of the Junior Detective League. When they split up to look for him, they discover a body, apparently killed by a hunter.

Then, as they flee, they find a bear cub tagging along with them!

The Deceitful Client

The beautiful kimono-clad Shizuka comes to the Mori Detective Agency with a missing persons request. However, her words are inconsistent and filled with lies, and Conan is suspicious. When they find the man she's looking for, he's already dead, clutching a picture of a younger Shizuka...

And There Were No Mermaids

Heiji invites Kogoro and company to Bikuni Island in the Wakasa Bay, known as "the Island of Mermaids." A local legend is that of a woman who became immortal after eating the flesh of a mermaid. On the day on which the 130-year-old Mikoto is to conduct the drawing of the Dugong Arrow, a murder occurs at the base of the waterfall!

Megure's Secret

Officer Sato is the decoy on an operation, but another woman is killed instead. Officer Sato insists that she can still play the part, but Inspector Megure refuses her. Megure's past is finally revealed...

The Mysterious Passenger

The Junior Detective League is on a bus trip. When a new passenger boards the bus, Ai Haibara senses the presence of one of the Black Organization. Conan attempts to contact the police, but one of the passengers is a lookout, and somehow, the Black Organization is involved...

The Evidence That Didn't Disappear

The Junior Detective League is invited to visit Professor Agasa's friend's house, where there are many dog lovers. When one of the dogs, Doyle, suddenly goes missing, his collar is discovered next to the incinerator. Is he really dead?

The Three Ks of Osaka Case

Three world-famous athletes open a restaurant together in Osaka, one of whom was a goalie that Conan looked up to. Then a murder occurs at the restaurant's opening party, and all three of them are suspects. They all had a motive, as the victim was a notorious sports journalist, but...

The Bullet Train Transport Case

Takagi and Sato are transporting a suspected drug dealer on the train when he gets away and is murdered. Will they be able to restore their honor?

The Gathered Detectives! Shinichi Kudo vs. Phantom Thief Kid

The Phantom Thief Kid has sent out another announcement! Kogoro Mori and five other detectives gather at the scene of the crime, and their personalities range from Miss Marple to Humphrey Bogart. This fabulous

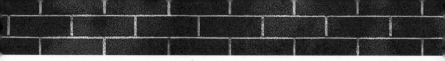

parody celebrates the thirtieth volume of the comic as all the detectives compete with one another to find the culprit.

Genta's Misfortune

Genta, unlike his usual self, doesn't finish his lunch one day. When the others ask him why, he says that someone is trying to kill him. Did Genta witness something?

The Murderous Pottery Class

Ran, Sonoko and Conan's pottery classroom is the scene of a murder! The suspect is the victim's life insurance beneficiary, her assistant. Conan, however, discovers evidence that this is not the case...

Kogoro Mori's Imposter

A countryside inn seems to be a popular place for suicides, and they hire Kogoro to come and check the contents of a suitcase.

When they get there, they discover a Kogoro imposter! It's all a joke until the imposter winds up dead...

Mystery Caught in the Trap

The Junior Detective League meets Ran and Sonoko on the beach and plays in an abandoned boat until they're chased off by a lifeguard. That night, a drowned corpse is discovered on the shore. How did the murder happen?

Osaka Double Mystery: The Swordsman and Taiko Castle (1)

Heiji's competing in his high school kendo tournament when he discovers a murder mystery at the university kendo tournament next door. The key to solving the mystery is finding out how the body was moved. Conan's arriving from Tokyo, but Heiji wants to solve this one himself. Will Conan get to it first?

Osaka Double Mystery: The Swordsman and Taiko Castle (2)

Conan's enjoying his tour, led by Heiji and Kazuha, when they encounter a history fan club at the castle. One of the fans dies by plummeting from the top of the castle, covered in flames. Meanwhile, Heiji's father, Heizo, appears and conducts a battle against a mysterious criminal group.

The Idols' Secrets

Yoko Okino invites Kogoro to her friend Kaoru Kusano's shower, where all the attendees are famous celebrities. When Kaoru doesn't return from her bath, her fiancé finds her with her neck slashed!

The Man from Chicago

The Junior Detective League attends an animal show, where they meet James Black. Later he's kidnapped by someone mistaking him for a millionaire. Conan quickly tracks him down, but...

Metropolitan Police Detectives Love Story 4

Officer Sato reluctantly agrees to meet a suitor her mother has found for her, but he turns out to be her coworker, Inspector Shiratori. If Takagi doesn't show by sundown, then she'll have to marry him, but Takagi's a little tied up chasing a convenience store robber...

The Truth Behind Valentine's

With Valentine's Day impending, Ran and Sonoko visit a chocolate-making club that promises to make their wishes come true. A sudden blizzard forces them to stay the night. Then one of the other lodgers is found clubbed to death and the corpse is covered in chocolate...

The Keepsake of a Crime

The Junior Detective League takes on one of Kogoro's cases, a request to find Mamorida's late wife's watch. During the investigation, Mamorida's neighbor

is watching a video — but later turns up dead! Conan suspects Mamorida, but how did he commit the crime when he's never even been in the room?

The Secret Rushed Omission

Miss Jodie invites Ran, Sonoko and Conan to a café , but she's been acting suspiciously! Suddenly, there's a blackout, and when the lights come back on, they find a corpse at the front of the café clutching a note that reads ○×△ .

English Teacher vs. Great Detective of the West

Still suspicious, Conan and Heiji visit Jodie's apartment, but Jodie merely welcomes them with a warm smile. While they're there, someone falls out of the apartment next door! The police rule it a suicide, but Conan and Heiji are sure there's something more going on.

The Hooligan in the Labyrinth

The Junior Detective League boards a train to go home after a soccer game when they encounter a soccer hooligan. When the crowded train clears, they find the hooligan stabbed to death! Conan quickly narrows down the suspects to three people, all of whom claim innocence. Which of them is lying?

Chinatown: Déjà Vu in the Rain

While enjoying dinner in Chinatown, the Mori family meets a producer who tries to recruit Ran into the acting biz. Suddenly, during dinner, the producer writhes in pain and dies. There's no poison in the food, so how did it happen?

Shinichi Kudo N.Y. (New York) Case

After the Chinese restaurant, Ran remembers the time she went to New York with Shinichi. They attended a Broadway musical with Yukiko and met a famous actress,

Sharon Vineyard. During the performance, one of the actors suddenly collapsed and died.

The Truth about the Ghost House

Kogoro and Conan investigate rumors of a haunted apartment. While waiting for the apartment's current resident, everyone suddenly falls asleep, and when they wake up they witness many strange phenomena. Ran screams in fear, but Conan detects a trick.

Mitsuhiko in the Forest of Indecision

Mitsuhiko misses his summer program, which is strange enough in itself, but then his family suddenly moves! The Junior Detective League is on the case, but all Mitsuhiko took with him was sun block and rice cakes wrapped in bamboo leaves.

The Solitary Island of the Princess and

the Dragon King

Kogoro Mori and Heiji Hattori go to Okinawa for a detective contest with the theme East vs. West. However, one of the staff members is murdered, causing Conan, Heiji and some others to be left behind on the island!

Malice and the March of the Saints

The Junior Detective League goes to watch a soccer team's victory parade when a terrorist sends out a bomb threat! Officers Sato and Takagi are on the lookout, but Takagi's car suddenly explodes! It seems the only clue is a video that Conan and his pals recorded...

The Trembling MPD: Twelve Million Hostages

A terrorist who sent out bomb threats seven and three years ago now sends out his third in a coded challenge: There are two bombs somewhere in Tokyo. Conan finds one of them, but like the incident in

which Officer Matsuda lost his life, the first bomb will notify them of the location of the second bomb only three seconds before it goes off! Can Officer Takagi and Conan protect Tokyo's 12 million inhabitants?

The Mystery Weapon

Kogoro's been asked to introduce a detective drama. He attends a filming, where he meets one of the actresses, Ruri, who happens to be an old schoolmate. While they reminisce about their past, one of the main cast members is murdered, and the murder weapon is nowhere to be found. It's a tough investigation, but Kogoro proves his worth.

The Remaining Voiceless Testimony

Three different people have come to Kogoro, asking him to find the same man: a programmer named Suguru Itakura. Conan discovers that Itakura was involved with the Black Organization, but by the time they find him, the man is already dead, and the evidence is gone with him...

Contact with the Black Organization: Negotiation, Pursuit, and Desperation

Conan obtains Itakura's diary and discovers that the Black Organization is looking for the software he developed. Since they don't know yet that Itakura is dead, Conan tricks Vodka into making a deal. While on the way to the place of the exchange, Professor Agasa's car stalls...

Festival Dolls at Sunset

The Junior Detective League helps decorate a home in hopes that they'll receive some ornamental dolls for Girls' Day. In the house is a scroll valued at 20 million yen. It is coveted by antiques collectors and traders. While everyone is out, someone steals the scroll! Can Conan figure out who did it?

The Hero with the Tarnished Mask

Kogoro and company hope to meet Wolface, a popular masked wrestler. But when Wolface's opponent is murdered in the waiting room, the security cameras show that Wolface was the one who did it!

Heiji Hattori's Desperate Situation!

Heiji and Kazuha are held prisoner by a lawyer who forces them to decode a certain cryptogram. The lawyer is an expert in tax evasion, and the evidence of this is in a locked safe, the password to which is in the cryptogram. When Heiji is late in meeting him, Conan gets suspicious...

The Red Horse in the Flame

A serial arsonist in Haidocho always leaves an ornamental horse at the scene of the crime. After someone dies in the fourth incident, a weak-willed antiques store owner turns himself in. It seems like the case is solved, but Conan and Heiji remember reading about a similar case in a novel...

A Priceless Friendship

The Junior Detective League goes camping once again, and they meet the Outdoor Club! Although they seem to be on good terms, Conan notices something suspicious. Then, one of the Outdoor Club members falls to his death!

A Small Client

Popular child actor Kazuki Kinukawa hires Kogoro to find his mother, who abandoned him years ago. He has only one clue as to her identity: a mole on her chest. Meanwhile, a murder in Atami points to a culprit who also has a mole on her chest...

Metropolitan Police Detectives Love Story 5

Takagi and Sato go on a date to Tropical Land, but Inspector Shiratori uses the narcotics squad to sabotage their date! Not only that, they end up having to look after the Junior Detective League, and overall the whole thing turns into a mess. But then drugs really do turn up in Takagi's bag, and it looks like they're on yet another case...

The Suspicious Curry

Kogoro and company rent a car to go to Sonoko's house, but the car gets washed into a river! Bad luck. They end up staying with a person named Akashi, who serves them curry for dinner. Ran and Conan bring some curry to Akashi's father-in-law, only to find that he's hanged himself in his room. According to the estimated time of death, Akashi could never have done it, but...

Gingko-Colored First Love

The Junior Detective League finds an old postcard from Professor Agasa's first love. It was sent 40 years ago and says that she'll wait under a certain maidenhair tree on a certain day of the year once every 10 years and today is one of those days! But Professor Agasa can't remember where the tree is. Will the Junior Detectives be able to help the professor?

Identical Princesses

Kogoro's thrilled that he just got a big job, but he spends the money before he's even solved the case! Now he has barely any clues. His ex-wife Eri and her high school friend Yukiko decide to take pity on him and help out.

The Secret of Tohto Film Developer

The Junior Detective League loves the Masked Yaiba movies, and thanks to Shinichi's mother, they're able to attend a premiere.

The reels are taking a long time to arrive, though, so they settle down for a nap. Meanwhile, one of the staff members is murdered. And not only that, but it looks like a mysterious car has been following Conan and Haibara!

Four Porsches

On their way back from taking Haibara to the clinic, Conan and company stop at the mall to eat some of the popular egg congee. Meanwhile, four Porsche owners gather in the underground parking lot. One of them dies...

The Secret Hidden in the Bathroom

Conan and Haibara visit an old friend of Haibara's father, hoping to find some clues about the Black Organization. But when they arrive at the agency, there's been another murder. Meanwhile, Vermouth of the Black Organization has wired Professor Agasa's house and is listening to his every word...

The Convenience Store Trap

Miss Jodie's leaving the school! When Ran and Sonoko ask her why, she just replies, "A secret makes a woman a woman!" When they go to a convenience store to get supplies for Miss Jodie's going-away party, the shop worker accuses them of shoplifting. Now that Conan and Shinichi aren't around, Ran has to show off her detective skills!

Head On Battle with the Black Organization: Two Mysteries Beneath the Full Moon

Vermouth of the Black Organization invites Kogoro Mori and Shinichi Kudo to a Halloween party on a Pacific Ocean cruise liner. Knowing full well that it's a trap, Conan accepts, and when a murder occurs, one of the party attendees takes off his costume— to reveal Shinichi Kudo underneath! Meanwhile, Miss Jodie appears to Haibara—at last, Jodie's, Sharon's and Chris's

secrets will be revealed!

Find the Mark on the Butt!

After school, Ayumi bumps into a suspicious man wearing a raincoat and comes away with a "5" marked on her hand. After the Junior Detectives investigate, the man gets away again, but not before Genta ends up with the same mark—on his butt!

The Forgotten Cell Phone

Kogoro's killing time in Café Poirot when the waitress asks him to return a lost cell phone to its owner. The owner turns out to be dead, and the cell phone is Kogoro's only clue. But what's with all these fake names and phone numbers?

The Deductive Show

Kogoro and company do some sightseeing in Osaka, but Heiji and Kazuha can't agree on where to take their guests. Kogoro suggests that he'll go with whoever solves a mystery first. Heiji gets Conan on his side, so it seems like they have the complete advantage, but then...

The Miracle at Koshien Park! The Defiants Face the Dark Demon

Conan and Heiji are watching the baseball finals at Koshien Park when Heiji picks up a cell phone and receives a call from a man calling himself the Demon of Koshien. If they don't find the phones that he'll ring at the end of the third, sixth and ninth innings, he'll commit suicide and take the 53,000 spectators with him! It all seems like a joke until a nearby warehouse explodes.

Metropolitan Police Detectives Love Story 6

There's a rumor that Officer Takagi's going to be dispatched to the Tottori Prefectural Police for a joint investigation. Officer Sato takes it calmly, but Takagi loses his

cool. Then a murder case involving their coworker Officer Chiba occurs!

Phantom Thief Kid's Miraculous Aerial Walk

Sonoko's relative and advisor to the Suzuki Conglomerate, Jirokichi Suzuki, has returned to Japan to challenge the Phantom Thief Kid and to restore his honor. Just try and steal the "Blue Wonder," Phantom Thief Kid!

Teitan High School Ghost Stories

Teitan High School is full of ghost stories, and Ran's afraid of ghosts! Conan investigates in an attempt to alleviate her fears and finds nothing spooky about the Gym Storage of Lamentation, the Library of Vengeance, or the Cursed Stairwell. But then he notices something...

Tragedy at the Pier in Plain Sight

Professor Agasa takes the Junior Detective League fishing, but the fish aren't biting. Things get a lot more exciting when one of the other anglers suddenly has trouble breathing. Is it poison? How can that be possible, when nobody's even gotten close to them?

The Silent Sea Route

Kogoro was going to interview pro pitcher "Jaguar" Nose, but Nose is murdered! Conan suspects Motoyama, former athlete-turned-TV personality, but he has an airtight alibi. Can Conan discover the truth?

A Code of Stars and Tobacco

The Junior Detective League is out stargazing in the mountains when they discover a body! Next to it is a cigarette case containing two short and two long cigarettes. Is this some kind of code?

The Dissonant Stradivarius

The sound from Vermouth's e-mail has been bothering Conan, but he can't quite put his finger on it. Then he hears that Kogoro's latest client is from a family of famous musicians who all have perfect pitch. It's been traditional that one of the family members plays a piece on the Stradivarius violin on the day of the family head's birthday—but lately, they've all been dying mysterious deaths!

Big Adventure in the Eccentric Mansion

The Junior Detective League goes camping again—and the Phantom Thief Kid makes another appearance! This time they're fighting over a mysterious treasure.

The Weird Family's Commission: Ran Suspects

Ran sends a text message to Shinichi that is received by Conan's cell phone! Kogoro's investigation of an affair turns into an investigation of murder. Ran's suspicion of Conan rises as the case proceeds.

The Red-Handed Jewel Thief

The Junior Detective League encounters Officer Takagi buying a ring for Sato. It's sheer bad luck that a robber enters the store right then! The robber jumps off a building in an attempt to evade Officer Takagi, but Conan notices that he seems really happy...

Conan and Heiji's Deductive Magic

Conan, Heiji and company attend a magic show. When Ran and Kazuha are invited to the stage, all four of them are invited to a backstage party with the other magicians. There's a sudden blackout, and when the lights come back on, there's a body on the floor...

The Shinto Shrine's Surprising Code

The Junior Detective League is supposed to be collecting insects, but they can't catch any! The Professor and Haibara create a cryptogram that even Conan can't crack, which makes them ecstatic. Then they receive a phone call for Shinichi from Ran. Looks like she and Sonoko have gotten mixed up in yet another murder...

The Evil Spirits that Appear on the Unlucky Day

Kogoro and company visit a wealthy man in Shizuoka who's supposedly been suffering from a curse for two years. Every year, on the unluckiest day of the Buddhist cycle, some misfortune befalls him. This year it's a murder, and the suspects are a strange group of people that suffer from everything from acrophobia to obsessive-compulsive disorder...

Black Impact! The Black Organization is Within Reach!

Newscaster Rena Mizunashi hires Kogoro to solve the mystery of his headaches. Conan solves it in a flash, but then he hears the melody that he heard when Vermouth sent a message to the Black Organization...

The Super Secret Road to School

Conan and the FBI were able to stop the Black Organization from assassinating an assemblyman, and they were able to take custody of organization member Kir. Conan returns to his daily life, where he hears about the disappearance of a fourth grader from his school...

The Irreversible Two

Eisuke Hondou, a boy who looks exactly like Rena Mizunashi, transfers into Ran's class. Though clumsy, he has a keen sense of observation. He's able to tell that Conan is extraordinary just by

watching him participate in one of Kogoro's investigations. Conan solves a locked-room case under Eisuke's scrutiny, but then...

Metropolitan Police Detectives Love Story 7

Kogoro and company go to a café where they see Officers Takagi and Sato on a group blind date. They don't want to disturb them, but then there's a kidnapping on the scene...

Interview with the Detective League

The Junior Detective League is going to be interviewed for a magazine article! They go with their homeroom teacher, Kobayashi, to the writer's house, only to find that he's been dead for half the day. Conan must now solve the case without arousing his teacher's suspicions...

Heiji's Memories

Heiji and Conan are talking on the phone. Heiji responds to one of Conan's jibes by saying he knows someone better even than Conan. Once, when he, Shinichi, Ran and Kazuha were in middle school, there was an incident with someone in the skiing class. So who's this detective that's even greater than Shinichi Kudo?

The Fish Mail Pursuit

Kogoro and company are approached by café Poirot waitress Azusa, who expresses her concern over an e-mail she received from a 5-year-old boy that read, "Will I be caught in the net like the other fish and die?" With this e-mail as their only clue, they now have to extricate this boy from a dangerous situation.

Digging for Clams While Sighing

The Junior Detective League is digging for clams in Shizuoka, where they meet a bunch of clam-digging enthusiasts from a local university. When one of them dies of cyanide poisoning, the police

rule it a suicide, but Conan thinks they should go digging again...

The Secret of the Russian Blue

Kogoro's ex-wife, Eri, wants Kogoro to take care of her Russian Blue cat, Goro, while she's gone. It's a chore, at least until Kogoro realizes that the cat's actions are related to the cryptogram he's been working on...

The Sealed Ocean Window

Conan, Ran and Eisuke are on their way to visit Sonoko's country house when they discover that the bridge is out. They visit a nearby house to use the phone, one that's owned by the members of an indie band. A murder occurs, and once again Eisuke's watching Conan...

The Premiere of Fate and Friendship

The Junior Detective League attends the premiere of a popular sci-fi movie series called Star Blade. While waiting in line, they are imitating the cast of the movies when a photographer takes their photo for a souvenir. But did he have an ulterior motive?

Metropolitan Police Detectives Love Story: The Fake Wedding

MPD Section 1 is guarding a bride and groom before their wedding. Messages have been sent by the culprit hinting that he'll attack on their wedding day. Officers Takagi and Sato take their place, but...

The Overturned Conclusion

A famous writer murders his apprentice and ghostwriter, and arranges the crime scene to give himself an alibi — an alibi that unravels when the Junior Detective League accidentally sends a baseball through his window...

Sonoko's Red Handkerchief

Sonoko and company visit a mountain made famous by the popular drama Winter Scarlet Maples. They try to reenact a scene from the drama by decorating the mountain with red handkerchiefs, but it looks like everyone else had the same idea! While they're there, they meet the assistant director, who later winds up dead. Sonoko's boyfriend, Makoto Kyogoku, makes a reappearance, the first in a long while.

Phantom Thief Kid and the Four Masterpieces

Phantom Thief Kid has sent another announcement: He's going to steal the four artworks that, when connected, become a world-famous masterpiece. While the police put their security into place, the artist's father-in-law is murdered! Is this the doing of Phantom Thief Kid?

Class 1-B's Great Operation!

Class has started, but Miss Kobayashi still hasn't arrived. However, there's a mysterious message on the blackboard: "We have Miss Kobayashi. Do you think you can find her? — Phantom With 200 Faces."

The Shadow of the Black Organization: The Young Witness and the Odd Evidence

Rena Mizunashi is still in a coma, but Conan's getting suspicious of Eisuke Hondou, who keeps hanging around the detective agency. Then a parent and child come to the agency. Supposedly, the child saw someone dump a body...

The Shadow of the Black Organization: The Mystery of the Big Reward and the Shining Star of Pearl

Eisuke Hondou has found an

interesting case on the Internet that bears some similarities to the Sherlock Holmes story "The Red-Headed League." Upon investigation, it seems to be connected to Kir's motorcycle accident. Did Eisuke plan this?

The Snowman That Cannot Be Smashed

The Junior Detective League is building snowmen in Gunma. Nearby, some college students are doing the same thing, and generally acting like little kids. When one of them is found dead in the lake below the cliff, Conan suspects foul play...

Three Days with Heiji Hattori (1)

The Mori family, along with Heiji and Kazuha, go cherry blossom viewing. Conan asks Heiji to see what he can find out about Rena Mizunashi. Meanwhile, a young monk claims to have seen a corpse disappear. The head monk at the temple, however, maintains that it was just a hallucination...

Three Days with Heiji Hattori (2)

Heiji tells Conan about a TV show called Detective Koshien, which features the Great Detective of the West, Heiji Hattori, and Saguru Hakuba taking Shinichi Kudo's place as the Great Detective of the East. There are also high school student detectives of the north and south, and the four of them compete. As things progress, however, a real murder occurs...

Genta's Deadly Shot

The Junior Detective League's favorite team lost! Genta puts all his frustration into kicking a ball in the parking lot. It flies off, and then they hear a scream. They find a German man who's collapsed and is now in critical condition. Is Genta to blame?

Shinichi Kudo's Childhood Adventure

When Shinichi and Ran were in the first grade, they investigated a

ghost in the library. A mysterious man handed them a coded message. Though Shinichi was young enough to still have trouble reading, he put his heart and soul into deciphering the message...

The Love of Eri Kisaki

Ran visits her mother at her law firm on the anniversary of her first date with Kogoro, where she sees her wedding ring in the trash. What's going on? Ran begins investigating...

Metropolitan Police Detectives Love Story 8: The Left Hand Ring Finger

The ring on Officer Sato's left hand ring finger is the talk of the station, but Officer Takagi isn't the one who gave it to her! Meanwhile, a famous mystery novelist that Kogoro was supposed to interview has been murdered.

The Mountain Witch's Blade

The Junior Detective League has set off on another camping trip when they blow a tire. They stay at the home of a woman who resembles a mountain witch, or yama-uba. Then a trio of two young men and a woman show up seeking shelter. That night, the woman is found murdered...

The Whereabouts of the Dark Photograph

Heiji Hattori's finally found some information on Eisuke Hondou! Someone recognized the photograph, but that person's computer has been wiped and there are signs of burglary in the house...

The Truth Behind the Mistaken Phone Call

Eisuke's father belonged to an organization called the Company. When Conan goes to inform Heiji of this, he ends up in the hospital—and finds Eisuke there too!

Murder Case from the Nether World

Rena Mizunashi is blood type AB. Eisuke Hondou is blood type O. They might not be related by blood. Conan and company decide to check out the house where Eisuke's mother supposedly works as a maid, and surprise, surprise, there's another murder.

The Devil at the TV Station

The Junior Detective League visits the TV station, where they meet rock star Satan Onizuka. Meanwhile, someone is murdered! You'd think Satan Onizuka would have a lot of trouble getting away with murder, with his elaborate costumes and makeup, but you'd be wrong…

The Fugitive

A one-shot from Kogoro's point of view. What's he running from?

Song of the Crow

Eisuke disappears after leaving a message that he found one of the members of the Company, to which his father belonged, at Haido Central Hospital. It turns out that the Company was one of the aliases of the CIA. After consulting with Jodie, he discovers that Eisuke's father was really Ethan Hondou. Conan goes straight to the hospital, but…

Akai's Past

The Black Organization has found out where Rena Mizunashi is being held! Shuichi Akai's really looking forward to meeting Gin of the Black Organization again. The war between the FBI and the Black Organization begins!

Friday the 13th

The battle with the Black Organization is over for the time being, and Conan returns to daily life. He attends a buffet with the Junior Detective League, where a murder occurs and FBI agent Camel is a suspect.

Beauty Salon Murder Case

Kogoro suspects that a hairdresser murdered her martial artist ex-boyfriend, but this hairdresser is also a friend of Eri! Could a woman really have committed this crime?

Furinkazan Murder Case

A wealthy family in Nagano Prefecture hires Kogoro to find out what really happened to their son, who was supposedly killed by a tornado. Kogoro and company get to know Inspector Kansuke Yamamoto of the Nagano Prefectural Police.

KEYWORD INDEX

G

H

I

J

M

N

O

P

Phantom Thief Kid	39 97 99
Pisco	70 140
Porsche 356A	68
Prof. Agasa	12 15 28
Public Servant Type 1 exam	58 122

Q

Queen of Justice	23

R

Rampo Edogawa	4 12 19
Ran Mori	8 17 134
Rena Mizunashi	89 91 95

S

Saitama	62 139
Sango Yokomizo	62 139
Seishi Yokomizo	107
Sergeant	57
Sharon Vineyard	73 75 99
Sherlock Holmes	109 120 154
Sherry	46 77 141

T